# The Coloured Pencil Artist's
# Drawing Bible

# The Coloured Pencil Artist's Drawing Bible

**Jane Strother**

Search Press

A QUARTO BOOK

Copyright © 2008 Quarto Publishing plc
This edition published in 2016 by
Search Press Ltd
Wellwood
North Farm Rd
Tunbridge Wells
Kent TN2 3DR

ISBN: 978-1-78221-396-3

Conceived, designed and produced by
Quarto Publishing plc
The Old Brewery
6 Blundell Street
London N7 9BH
www.quartoknows.com

QUAR: CPSB

Project editor: Emma Poulter
Art editor: Julie Francis
Copy editor: Hazel Harrison
Proofreader: Ruth Patrick
Indexer: Dorothy Frame
Photographer: Martin Norris
Managing art editor: Anna Plucinska
Art director: Caroline Guest

Creative director: Moira Clinch
Publisher: Paul Carslake

Colour separation by Modern Age Repro
House Ltd, Hong Kong.
Printed by Toppan Leefung Printing Ltd,
China.

# Contents

# Introduction

The primary role of an artist is one of communication and interpretation; the medium and the skills you acquire in handling it are the means through which you express your ideas and pictorial interests. Interpretation is a personal matter, and cannot be taught, but practical skills can, and the aim of this book is to provide you with a repertoire that allows you to make the most of your coloured pencils. But there are many different ways to draw and paint, and although practising methods and techniques can be stimulating and fulfilling, openness to experimentation and exploring options is often the best way to success. You as the artist have an influential role to play, and I hope that you will see this book as a stepping stone towards developing your own way of working.

Coloured pencils are an excellent medium for the newcomer to drawing and painting, and will be familiar to many through childhood 'colouring-in' exercises, but they can also produce highly sophisticated results, and the pencils used by artists today are a world away from the cheap and cheerful

***Techniques*** *Step-by-step demonstrations take you through the all-important techniques.*

crayons of the school room. Highly versatile, they can be used as a drawing or a painting medium, either on their own or in conjunction with other media.

**The Coloured Pencil Artist's Drawing Bible** is divided into several sections, starting with the basic tools and materials required, following on to a chapter on how to use them, each technique illustrated with clear step-by-step demonstrations by professional artists. Here you will find advice on basic drawing skills such as hatching, shading or blending as well as those with a more specialised use, such as burnishing or impressing. 'All about colour' offers insights into

***Pencil ranges***
*Types of coloured pencils and their use with a range of other media are discussed.*

*Colour* All aspects of colour theory are clearly explained.

colour relationships, and how you can use these to give your work additional impact. You will also learn how to mix colours, achieving many different hues with quite a small basic palette. 'Planning and Procedures' will help you decide how to compose your pictures, how to choose the best viewpoint and how to get the most out of your sketchbook studies.

The latter part of the book contains several full-scale demonstrations, allowing you to 'look over the artist's shoulder' to see how each one goes about their personal style of picture making and builds up their effects. This is followed by a gallery of finished works by a variety of artists, which bears testimony to the versatility of the medium and hopefully will give you ideas as to how to develop and enrich your own drawing style. Finally, the 'Subjects' section provides a wealth of possible drawing subjects with a selection of photographs divided into themes, along with advice on how you might translate them into coloured-pencil drawings.

All in all, **The Coloured Pencil Artist's Drawing Bible** is a must have for anyone interested in this medium, whether a beginner or a more experienced artist looking for new approaches.

# CHAPTER 1

# Tools and Materials

# Types of coloured pencil

The main difference between types of coloured pencil is whether or not they are water-soluble. The latter can be used wet or dry, providing a high degree of textural variation. Both these and any of the softer, waxier pencils create subtle shading effects and colour gradations.

Line work, hatching and shading with any degree of intricacy requires a finer pencil, which retains a sharp point for longer, even if the preliminary work is done with a water-soluble one. In fact, some of these pencils perform extremely well on a surface previously worked with water-soluble pencil – wet or dry.

Working with a combination of both types of pencil provides an opportunity for a greater range of marks and layering of colour, although the variations may be slight.

**Colour ranges** *There are a number of colour ranges available, and the pencils vary in character from chalky and opaque or soft and waxy, to hard and translucent. These variations are caused by the different proportions of binder – the substance that holds the pigment together.*

**Watercolour effects**
*Water-soluble pencils, such as those shown on the right, are easy and convenient to use. Used wet or dry, the pencils can be used to create a variety of effects from bold, vibrant colours to delicate watercolour washes.*

**Specific sets** *Sets of pencils can vary from as few as 12, to as many as 120. A good choice, initially, could be the special landscape and portrait sets, which include a balanced range of muted 'natural' colours in warm and cool hues, and light and dark tones.* Glimpse of the Harbour *(shown above) uses a fairly neutral 'drawing set' (shown right), specifically designed for both landscape and portrait work. The initial shading shows a grainy texture on cartridge paper, subsequent work binds the layers together producing the soft, creamy blend seen in the foreground, or the dark blue-brown of the house on the right.*

## ARTIST'S TIP

Pencils need to be sharpened regularly, so include a craft knife and a pencil sharpener in your tool kit. Generally the knife is the most useful as it stays sharp for far longer. The blade is made in sections, and when it becomes blunt, you simply remove the top section with a pair of pliers. Reserve the pencil sharpener for reclaiming points rather than for shaving off the wood.

# Paper types

The paper you choose will influence your drawing style, so it is important to go for something sympathetic to the marks you intend to make, or allow the paper itself to dictate a particular quality in your drawing.

Drawing (cartridge) paper is a good all rounder. It is relatively smooth, but has a slight tooth that gives a grainy quality to lighter strokes. With increased pressure, the grain will fill in, and either become less obtrusive or totally lose its effect. For fine or detailed work, a smooth surface is essential, but not too smooth. It is impossible to build up any density without some tooth to hold the pigment; pencils will skid on a shiny, slippery surface. As a rule, the more heavily textured the paper grain, the longer it stays open and allows the build-up of pigment.

*Pastel paper* The pronounced grain of pastel paper is evident in Moonlit Table. The regular patterned appearance is reflected in the flat, blocked-in shapes; a more detailed, fluid image would be less suitable for this paper.

*Drawing papers* From left to right: Absorbent heavyweights in green, cream, and two tones of buff (*1–4*); lightweight, mould-made Ingres paper (*5–6*); medium-weight, hot pressed papers in cream, green and grey (*7-9*); heavy, hot-pressed paper (*10*); rough white paper (*11*); rough paper with a pronounced tooth (*12*); handmade heavyweight paper (*13*); small-sized sketchbook (*14*).

1
2
3
4
5
6
7
8
9
10
11
12
13
14

# Drawing paper

This has a relatively smooth surface, but the texture can vary. The example shown here has a relatively defined grain; texture is evident even when heavy pressure is used. On a lighter-grained paper, texture will be less evident as the grain fills with pigment.

# Watercolour paper

Standard watercolour paper, known as cold-pressed, can be too heavily textured for coloured pencils – shading over the surface will leave the 'dips and troughs' free of pigment. The more suitable types have texture but little obvious grain, and will allow a considerable build-up of pigment when shaded.

# Coloured pastel paper

A relatively pronounced texture is needed to grip the loose, powdery pigment. This paper would not be suitable for detailed coloured-pencil work, but works well for some styles, for example, those used in *Moonlit Table* on page 12.

# Shiny paper

If the paper is too smooth, the pigment simply sits on the surface. If you try to deepen a pale colour, you will see an immediate waxy build-up wherever heavy pressure has been used, reminiscent of children's wax crayons.

# Paper painted with acrylic primer

The brushmarks used to apply the primer create a coarse texture that tends to break up pencil strokes. Applications of water-soluble pencils dissolved in water can give very rich results; the surface holds the pigment but doesn't absorb it, and the bright white quality enhances the translucency.

# Sketchbooks

Sketchbooks or pads come in all shapes and sizes; softback, hardback, landscape or portrait format, spiral bound or with a sewn binding. The quality of the paper will vary so check details on the label giving weight and texture. What you buy depends on your purpose; for quick sketches in the field, something smallish with a hard back would be a good choice, and for exploratory studio work a larger one, with easily removed sheets.

**Hard-backed**
*Many people are attracted to these seductive hard-backed, blank books just asking to be filled with your thoughts and ideas, drawings and writings.*

**Sewn-in bindings** *Sewn-bound sketchbooks are made in many shapes and sizes, and usually have either printed marbled covers or black canvas ones. They are more expensive than spiral bound pads, but are substantial enough to last for a long time.*

**Spiral-bound pads** *These are easy to use, as the paper lies flat. Choose one with a heavy backing that acts as a support to lean on. The binding can be an obstacle, however, especially if you want to work on a double-page spread, and a flimsy front cover won't protect it from becoming dog-eared in your backpack.*

## ARTIST'S TIP

If out and about, keep a small sketchbook to hand – in the event that inspiration strikes, it's good to be prepared. Remember to keep a bulldog clip handy too – you'll need to secure those pages on a windy day!

# Different sizes

Whether sewn-in or spiral-bound sketchbooks are your thing, keep several sizes and shapes for specific needs or to record separate trips and projects. Sewn binding has the added advantage of allowing a drawing to cover a double page spread, an option worth considering.

**Formats** Landscape and portrait format hardback sketchbooks with sewn binding.

# Stretching paper

Paper is made in different weights, expressed as grams per square metre (gsm) or lbs per ream. If water is to be applied to the surface, or a wet pencil is used, all but the heaviest need to be stretched to avoid buckling. There are two ways of doing this, and artists have their own personal preferences. You can either soak the paper on both sides in a bath, lift it out by a corner and shake off the excess before placing it on a board and sticking paper tape around the edges, or you can wet one side only. Some artists complain that the surface is stirred up when soaked; to others this can be an expedient. For drawing and mixed-media work, soaking the whole sheet when stretching can be an advantage. It changes the nature of the drawing surface and facilitates a superb line quality.

Once your paper is stretched and dry, you can prime it with primer (see page 56) or apply any other sort of ground or colour you wish (see page 45 for more about colouring paper).

**ARTIST'S TIP**

Stretching paper in a sketchbook is obviously not possible, but in the case of a sewn-binding sketchbook you can help to prevent the paper buckling by applying a wash to pages, allowing them to dry thoroughly, and then closing the book and weighting it overnight.

**1** Prepare four strips of adhesive-paper tape, approximately 50 mm (2 inches) larger than the paper.

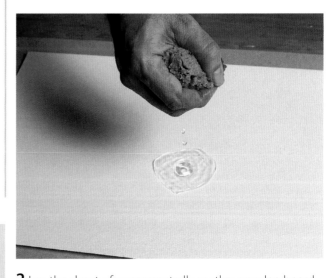

**2** Lay the sheet of paper centrally on the wooden board and wet it thoroughly, squeezing the water from the sponge. Alternatively, the paper can be wetted by holding it under a running tap, or by dipping it into a water-filled tray or sink.

**3** Wipe away any excess water with the sponge, taking care not to distress the paper surface.

**4** Beginning on the longest side of the paper, wet a length of tape using the sponge, and lay it down along the edge. Ensure that about one-third of the tape surface is covering the paper, with the rest on the board.

**5** Smooth the tape down with the sponge. Apply the tape in the same way along the opposite edge and then along the other two edges. Place the board and paper aside to dry for a few hours, or use a hairdryer to speed up the drying process, but keep the dryer moving so the paper dries evenly, and do not hold it too close to the paper's surface.

**6** Staples can be used to secure medium- and heavyweight papers. Wet the tape and position it on the board, as above. Secure the edges by placing staples at regular intervals, working quickly before the paper buckles.

# Essential tools

The beauty of coloured pencils as a medium is that few additional tools are needed for studio work, and even less for outdoor sketching. A list of items for outdoor work is given on page 87. For studio work, you will usually require a larger range of pencils than for sketches, though don't go overboard and buy a vast range (see the suggestions for a basic palette opposite). If you are interested in mixed-media work, you may wish to have other media such as inks and watercolours to hand, and you may also want to experiment with different kinds of paper.

If you like to work on a large scale, you will need a drawing board, which can be just a piece of furniture board cut to size. An easel is not essential, but you may find that it encourages you to work more freely. You may also need some form of lighting if your work space is not adequately lit, or if you are working outside the daylight hours. There are many inexpensive adjustable table lamps available, and you can also buy special daylight bulbs in most art stores.

### Erasers
*Erasers can be used as a drawing tool, as well as to make corrections. The type of eraser you choose depends on your paper: a kneadable eraser for smooth papers and a firmer plastic eraser for more textured types.*

*Kneadable eraser*

*Plastic eraser*

### Drawing board
*The working surface you choose depends very much on how large you want to work, but most artists use a drawing board of some kind, whether a ready-made one or a sheet of medium-density fibreboard (MDF).*

### Anglepoise lamp
*If you are not blessed with good natural light, or want to work in the evening, you will need a good lamp. Angelpoise lamps are ideal, because they are adjustable and can be changed to different heights and angles.*

# Basic palette

A suggested basic palette for coloured-pencil work would generally include two or three versions (or hues) of each of the primary colours – red, yellow and blue. Remember to include some darks and lights to add tonal value to your work.

There are several variations you may want to include in your palette: lemon, cadmium and ochre as variants of yellow; ultramarine, turquoise, cerulean and indigo as a choice of blues; and scarlet or vermilion, and magenta or crimson, for differing shades of red. An olive green, burnt sienna and a pastel pink are also useful additions. It is also a good idea to include some neutral colours such as browns and greys.

**On the move**
*The suggested basic palette for taking on trips out, from top to bottom: cool pink (**1**), magenta (**2**), vermilion (**3**), French grey (**4**), lemon yellow (**5**), cadmium yellow (**6**), yellow ochre (**7**), raw sienna (**8**), olive green (**9**), light turquoise (**10**), spectrum blue (**11**) ultramarine (**12**) and indigo (**13**).*

1
2
3
4
5
6
7
8
9
10
11
12
13

**Sketchbooks**
*You should stock up on a range of sketchbooks of different sizes and formats.*

# CHAPTER 2

# Techniques

# Handling pencils

There is no right or wrong way to hold a coloured pencil; any grip that is comfortable and gives you control of the pencil movement is right for you. However, you may vary your hand grip depending on the nature of the paper, the area to cover and the direction of the marks you intend to make, and thus the effects you obtain will vary subtly as you alter your grip and pressure.

The conventional grip in which the shaft of the pencil rests in the curve of the thumb and first two fingers gives tight control and enables you to make very delicate marks, firm lines and careful shading by small movements of the fingers, wrist or hand.

For more open, scribbled or hatched textures use more sweeping movements of your hand and arm. Alternatively, grip the pencil with your hand either over or under the shaft, which encourages free, gestural movements. Shading with the underhand grip can be light and quick, and with the overhand one, heavy and vigorous – especially if you stand at an easel or at a tilted board.

## Using an easel

Working at a sturdy easel encourages full use of the arm as well as the wrist and so facilitates sweeping movements, more flowing marks and perhaps heavier pressure. Perspective is often easier to judge, particularly vertical and horizontal structures as you are working on the same plane.

*The 'writing' grip*
*Use this conventional grip for maximum control where extreme precision is required.*

*The underhand grip*
*This grip will facilitate free movement of the wrist, and is ideal for open shading.*

## WORKING POSITION

Your choice of working position depends greatly on how large you want to work. If you are not using an easel, then a drawing board is a good idea. Propped up on some wooden blocks, or against a table as shown here, an angled board is ideal for drawing, and can help with your posture too. Always ensure you are sitting comfortably – an adjustable chair is a good idea, especially for those with back problems. But regardless of the type of chair you use, try to stand up regularly and avoid spending long periods of time hunched over your work.

### The overhand grip

*Heavier, more gestural marks can be made with this grip.*

### Wrist movement

*Curves and ellipses are more easily created if your wrist is allowed to move freely. Here the wrist has twisted from a position in line with the hand to one almost at right angles.*

# Mark-making: Dry pencils

Marks are the means through which you record and translate your visual experiences, so before launching into drawing an actual subject from life or memory, gain familiarity with your materials. You could divide your page with a grid similar to the one shown here, or allow yourself to freely roam over the page. Become absorbed in the lines, dots, shading and the relationships between colours you produce – and the differences between brands, if you are using more than one.

*1 Loose, scribbled marks and a medium pressure on watercolour paper.*

*2 Loose, shaded marks with a slightly heavier pressure on watercolour paper.*

*3 Sharp point and medium pressure on smooth drawing paper.*

*4 Sharp point and medium pressure on drawing paper stained with thin oil pastel.*

*5 Dense crosshatching in one colour on smooth drawing paper.*

*6 Dense, scribbled marks in several colours, overlaid and blended. This decreases their intensity and enhances the flashes of orange.*

*7 Firm, even pressure on smooth drawing paper.*

*8 The grain of the paper filled with layers of the same blue.*

*9 Fine scratched marks add further subtlety to heavy shading on textured paper.*

*10 Firm pressure on heavy, smooth drawing paper.*

*11 Short, energetic hatched red marks on a complementary lime green.*

*12 Loose shading in harmonious pinks and reds on textured paper.*

*13 Vibrant dark tones created by dense layering of blue, red and yellow.*

*14 Light shading in blue and yellow to produce green.*

*15 Close, linear hatched marks in different colours to produce a blended effect.*

*16 Colour densely shaded over impressed marks (see page 36) on smooth drawing paper.*

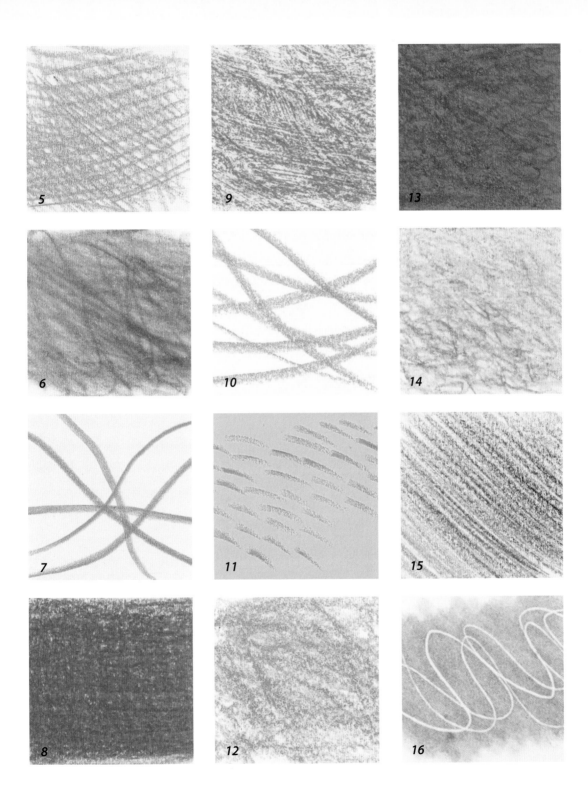

# Hatching

Hatching and crosshatching are blending techniques, traditionally used to build up areas of tone in monochrome drawings using a linear medium, such as pen and ink drawing or engraving. In coloured pencil work, these methods are an effective way to mix colours or to modify them.

Hatched lines are roughly parallel and can take any direction. Heavy lines, closely spaced, give a fairly solid area of tone or colour, appearing more dense than widely spaced, light lines. Crosshatching is simply two or more sets of lines hatched one over another in different directions. An area of dense crosshatching would read, from a distance, as a continuous tone or colour. The direction of the lines can be carefully manipulated to represent form and volume or loosely massed to give a lively surface or sense of movement.

Working in line only does not have to be restrictive. It can be a very free and unencumbered way of drawing from life, as there is plenty of scope for redrawing or adjusting marks by overlaying new ones, gradually building up a more complex finished piece.

## Regular hatching

Hatched lines can be of equal weight and spacing or may vary with gradual alteration in thickness and spacing.

*Evenly spaced hatched lines of equal weight.*

*Lines of varying thickness, spacing and weight.*

***Free hatching*** *Worrying about the precise direction and spacing of hatching and crosshatching can sacrifice the sense of life and energy in a drawing, so free yourself with some quick studies such as the apple and pear shown here. The pencils have been allowed to move easily following the form of the fruit, and the directional marks have been extended into the background for added dynamism.*

# Crosshatching

The denser texture of the closely crossed lines allow you to develop deeper and livelier colour as the white of the paper is gradually eliminated.

*Hatched and crosshatched lines can be used to effectively blend two or more colours.*

*This loosely hatched and crosshatched sketch uses change in pressure to alter the tonal balance.*

*Hatched lines can be loosely massed to give a lively surface or a sense of movement.*

# Blending

Blending one colour into another is generally achieved by shading – using the side of the pencil and moving it back and forth across the paper. This leaves a softer, more open mark than the point, especially on grainy paper, which can be gradually blended into an adjoining colour by subtly overlapping the edges of the two colours so that neither is dominant and there is no discernible join. This is known as feathering.

## Blending two colours

An effective blend is made by loosely shading over an existing colour of a similar hue or tone; the two mingle and appear as a blend although there are two distinct layers. This is more pronounced when shading on previously coloured paper with a grain, as the pigment sits on the surface and leaves the 'dips' in the lower sheet free – the eye will blend two colours used in this way, achieving a lively surface quality.

*Blending with an even light pressure and no linear bias.*

*Blending with heavy pressure for increased intensity of colour and tone with emphasis in the direction of shading.*

*Feathering using light and moderate pressure in one direction to blend two colours.*

**Blending by unifying**
The effect of sunlight in Formal Garden *shown left, is emphasised by shading with yellow over large patches of previously worked colour. This helps to pull the composition together, brightening even the shaded areas. The watercolour paper used for the drawing is soft, with no obvious grain, which aids the merging of the pencil strokes, seen particularly in the light and shade of the hedge in the background.*

◀ **Working on dark paper**
*The seascape shown opposite, Dinas Head, has been worked on black paper, with yellows and pinks blended by means of shading and heavy pressure to cover the paper. The colours appear light on the dark ground, evoking a quality of light characteristic of this coastal area.*

## OPEN SHADING

This is the result of loose movement of the wrist, which allows the whole hand rather than just the fingers to manipulate the pencil and to produce free, descriptive marks over the whole picture surface. This method might be used to build up basic shapes in the first draft of a picture subsequently to be worked up in depth, and is a good way to eliminate unwanted tightness at the beginning of a project.

# Blending with solvents

The marks made with some types of coloured pencil can be blended with solvents – water, turpentine or the spirit-based medium in a colourless marker blender. Only pencils formulated to be water-soluble will react with water. Spirit solvents may dissolve the colours of pencils intended to be used dry – this has to be a matter of experiment, as it depends on the proportions of the pigment and binding materials in the pencil lead, and the effects are not wholly predictable.

There are two methods that enable you to take advantage of the more fluid textures produced by solvent techniques. You can either dip the tip of the pencil into the solvent, so that the colour becomes softened and spreads as you lay it down; or you can shade or hatch with a dry pencil tip and work into the colour area with the solvent using a brush, paper stump (torchon), or cotton bud – or with a marker blender, which is simply a marker pen that contains a colourless solvent. You can combine the effects of wet and dry colour by allowing the dampened marks to dry, then reworking the area with the pencil.

To avoid distortion that may occur through the paper buckling when it is wetted by the solvent, stretch the paper beforehand, or work on a pre-stretched paper block or board.

**ARTIST'S TIP**
Unless you use very thin paper, no stretching is required when working with solvents, as they don't buckle the paper like water does. But bear in mind that spirit or turpentine can stain coloured paper, and if using a marker blender, the tip needs to be kept clean or it may become contaminated and dirty future blending.

## Using spirit solvent

**1** The shapes of the flowers are rapidly sketched with a soft, waxy pencil line. A rag dampened with turpentine is used to spread the colour delicately, indicating the areas of darkest shading.

**2** The line drawing is strengthened and some broad colour areas blocked in with light shading. Notice the heavy grain of the watercolour paper – when applying solvent, you need to use good-quality paper to avoid buckling or tearing.

**4** To develop the intensity of colour, pencils are used once more to shade in the solid shapes. The moisture from the underlayers makes the pencil marks smoother and more vibrant.

**3** A second stage of rubbing with turpentine softens the colour and spreads it into the paper grain. The pencil marks are just moistened, not flooded with the solvent.

**5** Applying solvent with a brush makes the colour dissolve and spread more like paint. It is possible to do this selectively, to build up a contrast of different textures.

**6** In the finished vignette, the brushed colour comes up very fresh and intense, contrasting nicely with the more open surface qualities of the pencil shading and line work.

# Blending water-soluble pencils

Water-soluble pencils are wonderfully versatile, as they can be used both wet and dry, or a combination of the two, in any one drawing. Apply water with a brush, rag or fine mist spray after the pencil is applied, and some of the pigment will dissolve, leaving soft and hard edges. Adding more water may even remove the drawing element completely to produce a watercolour wash effect. You can wet the paper before drawing, or dip the tip of the pencil in clean water to give a soft line.

It's advisable to stretch your paper (see page 16) unless it is the heaviest watercolour paper, but if you plan to use a limited amount of water, just enough to dampen the paper, try attaching it to a board with masking tape on all sides. This is a good method for instant sketches.

## ARTIST'S TIP

There are many types of brushes you can use. As you become more experienced, you will begin to learn which type of brush works best for you. Remember: a good brush should have a certain resilience. You can test the spring of a brush by wetting it into a point and dragging it lightly over your thumbnail. It should not droop but spring back.

## Blending more than one colour

Lay down two dry colours one on top of the other and wash with water – once you have blended them there is little significant difference as to the order in which they are laid. Differences are more discernable when dry pencils are laid over each other, as you will see below.

*The crimson (top right) slightly dominates the viridian when laid on top, although these two hues are similar in tone, as is evident when the colours are laid the other way round (top left). There is little difference once washed over.*

*Yellow over purple (top left) looks quite different to purple over yellow (top right) because of the contrast in tonal value between the two. However, the differences are not so evident once they are washed with water (see bottom row).*

*Red over lime green (top left) and lime green over red (top right) are tonally very similar, but there is a slight change in hue. Again, the differences in hue, and the order in which they are laid, are less apparent once washed with water.*

# Blending with water

Blending with water, using a brush, sponge or rag, allows subtle mixtures and varied line quality to be achieved.

**1** A swatch is made using a dry pencil.

**2** Water is added with a brush and the colour is blended more thoroughly, loosing most of the pencil marks.

Dipping the pencil in water first produces different marks. Where the pigment is wet, it makes a deeper and stronger mark that tails off as it dries.

### Watercolour effects

*This drawing,* Chinese Dishes, *was begun with a rough sketch blocked in with shading, much of which was then dissolved using water and a brush to create a fluid watercolour painting. It was then reworked with drawn lines and some loose shading to emphasise shape and form, and the process was then repeated. The stages are integrated so that it is not always possible for the viewer to identify the order in which they were made.*

# Mark-making: Water-soluble pencils

Using water-soluble pencils will give a different appearance to the marks you make. Depending on your approach, your finished work might resemble a watercolour painting rather than a drawing, with few visible pencil marks, or alternatively you might choose to employ the contrast between water-blended areas and pencil texture. Use the examples shown here as a starting point for your own experiments until you feel you can use the medium with confidence to describe and interpret your subject.

*1 Wet, red pencil with heavy pressure over dried water-blended colour.*

*2 Red acrylic ground allowed to dry and overlaid with blue pencil blended with water. The red and the blue will not mix.*

*3 Yellow overlaid with green and softened with a wet brush.*

*4 Colour spread with water to produce a thinned and lightened blue.*

*5 Red-stained paper with water-blended blue laid on top and then scratched with a craft knife to reveal the underlying colour.*

*6 Scribbled wet pencil marks lightly meshed together.*

*7 Scribbled, soft marks made with a pencil dipped in water.*

*8 Two colours begin to blend with solvent in the form of a marker pen.*

*9 Impressed marks (see page 36) on red-stained paper with shaded overlay in green.*

*10 Scribbled marks blended with water and allowed to 'pool' as in watercolour.*

*11 Blue blended with red on grainy paper. The marks have been softened but still remain visible.*

*12 Dry pencil over a previous layer of water-blended blue.*

*13 Marks on wet paper, coloured with a pencil wash.*

*14 Marks on dry paper with water brushed over the surface afterwards.*

*15 Texture created by layering wet and dry pencil marks.*

*16 Wet pencil loosely scribbled over commercially made coloured paper.*

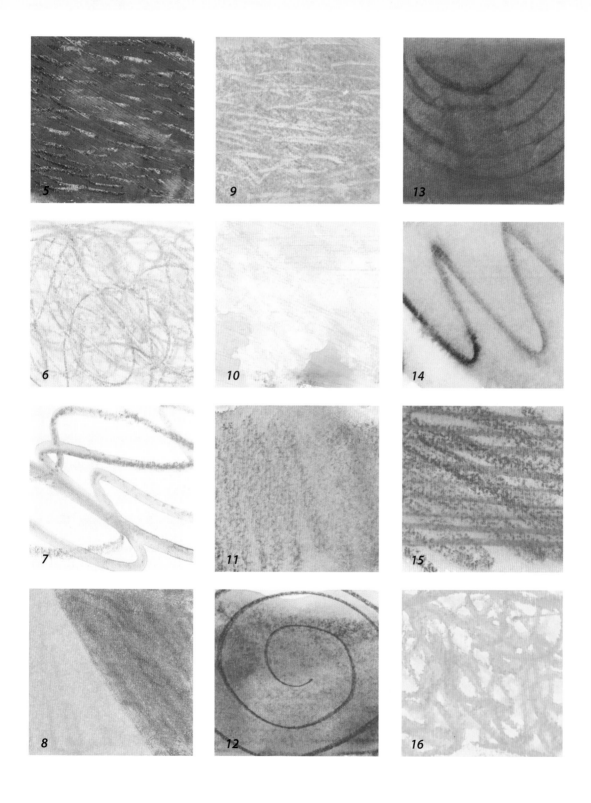

# Impressing

This is a way of producing clean 'negative' lines in a drawing by indenting the paper. When worked on white paper, it is also known as 'white line drawing'. Lay a sheet of good-quality drawing paper or a smooth watercolour paper on a pad made from a few sheets of newspaper to provide the necessary yielding surface, and use an implement such as a 'dead' ballpoint pen or, a knitting needle or the end of a paintbrush handle to impress lines. Subsequent gentle shading will glide over the impressed mark, revealing the colour of the paper. For a varying effect, use a sharpened coloured pencil to make the lines, so the impressed line will be of that colour rather than that of the paper.

## Using tracing paper

Impressing can be done freehand, but if the drawing is complex, you can make it first on tracing paper, laying this over a clean sheet of drawing paper and retracing the outlines firmly with a pencil point. Impressing can be used to create specific decorative effects such as the patterns in a fine lace tablecloth, the delicate tracery of leaf veins, or simply as a negative outline in white or the chosen paper colour.

**1** Place a sheet of tracing paper over your chosen design and make a pencil tracing of the whole image.

**2** Remove the tracing paper from the image, lay it over your drawing paper and redraw the lines to be impressed using a ballpoint pen or pointed implement.

**ARTIST'S TIP**
It is useful to keep one or two alternative impressing 'tools' for different thicknesses of line; a compass point will give a finer negative line than a paint brush handle.

**3** Remove the tracing paper. Using the side of the pencil, shade over the impressed surface to reveal white lines.

**4** The shading can be taken a stage further to include more than one colour, but make sure that the impressed lines are kept free of colour.

**▲ White line drawing**
This crane design is taken from a nineteenth-century Japanese fabric. The white lines are made by tracing the image with a ballpoint pen, impressing a 'blind' line onto smooth white drawing paper.

**▶ Negative outline**
The poppy design uses an impressed white line as an outline, shaded lightly all over in pink before the green was added. The poppy head was shaded again in red before further impressing to give the fine, broken lines on the petals.

# Sgraffito

Sgraffito is the technique in which an underlying layer is revealed by scratching or scraping the top one away. It works particularly well when the media is soft and easily removed, as with oil paint or oil pastel. Coloured pencils tend to mesh together when overlaid and impregnate the surface of the paper rather than sit on the top, so care should be taken to avoid damaging it. However, sgraffito is reasonably successful when the pigment is compacted and on smooth or primed paper. Use the point for fine lines or scrape lightly with the side of the blade for broken areas.

Try representing the flicker of light penetrating dark foliage, the sky through tangled branches, a complex textured surface or a distinctive linear structure, such as basket weave, waving corn or the fragile veins of a leaf skeleton.

## Scraping out

Removing colour with a knife by scraping with the edge of the blade rather than the point, can be used to clear unwanted pigment build-up in order to rework or to create striking 'negative' line drawing.

**1** Use a coloured pencil to build up an area of compacted colour.

**2** Here a second hue is added to deepen the colour and to increase its density.

**3** Use a craft knife to carefully scrape away fine lines or patches of colour, so the white of the paper or the pigment underneath is revealed. Use the flat part of the blade rather than digging into the paper with the point.

**▼ Fine lines**

*Here fine lines are scratched into compacted
pigment to emulate delicate leaf veins. The
effect is reinforced with further gentle shading
over the scratch marks; anything too heavy
and they would fill in.*

**▲ Revealing colours**

*Merriscourt Farm – High Summer has been
worked on primed paper, with sgraffito used to
take out some of the dark tree mass on the
extreme left to reveal the yellows and pinks
beneath. Fine scratched hatching adds variety
and detail to the straw bales and the barley field.*

### ARTIST'S TIP

For good results, prime the stretched
paper (see page 16) with an acrylic or
gesso primer or a layer of acrylic paint
(see pages 56–57). This acts as a barrier
between the pencil and the paper,
preventing it from absorbing the pencil
colour. The top colour can be scraped
away with a craft knife to reveal white
or coloured marks.

# Burnishing

Burnishing is used to give an overall finish to a drawing, to heighten selected areas or to imitate shiny materials such as metal or glass. It is difficult to make radical changes to a burnished area once established, although it can be removed with water (if you are using water-soluble pencils) or broken up by scraping with a craft knife or even glasspaper.

To burnish with a coloured pencil, apply a top layer to a previously worked area, using firm pressure so that the colour is compacted and no grain is evident. This creates a smooth, blended surface, increasing brightness and reflectivity. The choice of hue adds a warm or cool bias to the subject, and also either heightens or subdues the colour. Use a white or pale pencil for highlights and rejuvenate dark areas by burnishing with a relatively lighter or brighter colour.

## Effects of burnishing

Burnishing with a coloured pencil creates a glazed surface effect. It compresses and polishes the first layer, pressing out the grain. It can give the impression of colours being more smoothly blended and increases the brightness and reflectivity of the surface. The colour applied affects the original hue, as shown below, where the same red colour has been subjected to several burnishing effects.

*Dense shading in red pencil.*

*The same colour burnished with blue-grey.*

*The same colour burnished with light yellow.*

*Red is burnished with white.*

*Burnished with a torchon.*

*Highly compacted red, orange and blue, partially burnished with white.*

## HOW TO MAKE A BURNISHING TOOL

To make a burnishing tool, you need a toothpick and a small piece of kitchen paper. Soak the paper in water and then roll it around the stick, without letting the paper protrude too far beyond the points of the stick. The paper will shrink as it dries to form a tight covering, without the need for further adhesion. Your paper stump is then ready for use.

**Burnishing using a tool**
*Half of the coloured patch has been burnished by rubbing with a paper stump (torchon) to achieve a compacted and shiny effect.*

**First of the season**
*Heavy pressure with a variety of red pencils was used for the four strawberries and then burnishing. From left to right, burnishing with white pencil, with yellow pencil, silver-grey pencil, with a paper stump (torchon) and with light yellow in the darkest areas of the background.*

### ARTIST'S TIP
Try burnishing with a rolled-paper stump (torchon) or a plastic eraser, to avoid the colour changes caused by overlaying colours.

# Working on coloured paper

Colours and tones can only be judged in relation to each other, so the appearance of your pencil colours will inevitably be affected by the paper colour. Red marks on a blue paper, for example, will look very different to the same marks on yellow paper. This applies even to 'white' paper, which is always lighter in tonal value than the lightest pencil colour, thus making the marks appear a little darker in contrast, especially if the white plays a dominant part in the work. Colours blended with water are brighter on white paper than they are on a coloured or tinted ground.

You can buy various coloured papers, but it can be more satisfactory to hand colour them yourself. You can lay washes of watercolour or thin acrylic, but remember that the paper must be stretched in advance or it will buckle (see page 16). The choice of colour depends very much on the subject and how you propose to treat it. You might choose a colour that blends with the landscape you are working from, perhaps a pale cool blue for early morning light, or a contrasting colour, such as red or yellow ochre for warm earth tones to enhance a predominately green landscape and bring it to life.

## Coloured-paper effects

A coloured ground affects the appearance of the pencil colour through contrast, enhancing or altering the different qualities of the colour to a greater or lesser extent. Neutral tints such as beige, buff or grey provide a mid-toned background and make good all-round choices; brightly coloured paper will make a strong impact on the overall image, intensifying the hue and texture of the pencil marks, but be aware that a particularly vivid background may compete with the applied colours. The swatches on the opposite page show the varying effects a coloured background can have on a colour's appearance.

**Neutral ground** *On this pale grey ground the colours retain their identity, though the colours that are close in tone to the paper show up less clearly.*

**Warm ground** *The warm yellow ground enhances and lightens the more translucent yellow, pink and cool grey swatches.*

**Cool ground** *The cool blue ground shown here deepens and brightens the raw sienna, darkens the red and raw umber and gives a slightly green tinge to the yellow.*

**Dark ground** *The colours all appear lighter on the darker, terracotta ground, but its intensity reduces the contrast, especially of the red, violet and the raw umber.*

### Inexpensive paper

Towards Reydon *is worked in dry pencil in cool blues and pinks on warm-toned brown sugar paper. This kind of paper can inhibit the build-up of layers, as the colour quickly becomes compacted, and too much erasing will tear the surface. However, you may find that you can develop your work by changing the type of pencil used for the final layer – the new pencil will often adhere more successfully.*

**Bright-coloured ground** *There is an almost luminous quality to this vignette in dry pencil on bright pink paper. Full use of complementaries or near-complementaries (see page 70) is seen in the use of the cool pink with the green of the beans and warm yellow lemon. The paler colours (pigment mixed with white) have a greater opacity than the others and so are less affected by the ground colour, thus adding to the vibrancy.*

# Colouring your own paper

Colouring paper yourself allows you to choose the exact hue you want and to modulate it to allow for a dense ground in one area and lighter in another. You can use oil pastel, or acrylic paint as shown below, or even stain your paper with a used tea bag.

**1** Squeeze a small amount of acrylic paint in your chosen colour onto a plate or palette and mix it with a brush loaded with a generous amount of water. For a more fluid consistency, you may need to add more water to enable the paint to spread easily over the paper surface.

**2** Using a brush, spread the paint over the paper, adding more water to the palette if necessary. Be sure to work quickly – If the paint starts to dry, hard edges will begin to occur.

**3** As you are painting, you will notice the brush marks are apparent. These can be either left as they are or smoothed out as shown in step 4 if they are too dominant.

**4** While the paint is still wet, use a damp rag to spread the paint further to the edges of your paper and smooth out some of the brush marks. Once dry, your paper is ready to work on.

# Transferring a sketch

With some types of coloured pencil drawing it is important to have a clear and accurate guideline before you begin the colour work. Corrections and erasures in the under-drawing can spoil the paper surface, so to avoid this, make a working drawing which can be transferred via tracing paper to the final drawing paper. Or, if you are working from a photograph or an existing drawing, you can enlarge or reduce it on a photocopier, and then trace the outlines. Alternatively, you can scan the image into your computer and use the scanning software to make any necessary alterations before printing out, but this would limit you as to size.

## Transfer paper

A quicker and cleaner method is to use transfer paper, which is similar to carbon paper but is made in a range of colours, and thus has the advantage of allowing you to choose a suitable colour. Slip the transfer paper coloured side down between the tracing and the drawing paper, and then draw over the outlines lightly.

## The tracing method

The conventional method of transferring a sketch simply involves using a piece of tracing paper and a coloured pencil.

**1** Draw the outlines on tracing paper, and then scribble on the back with a graphite pencil, coloured pencil, soft pastel or chalk

**2** Place the tracing paper onto the drawing paper and go over the outlines again with a ball point pen or sharp pencil to transfer the image.

# Resizing your image

If you don't have access to a photocopier to enlarge or reduce an image, you can do it by hand, as shown below. This is a slow method, but it is good practice, helping to sharpen your observation and drawing skills. All of these methods, however, are essentially devices for copying. Practise enlarging or reducing by eye to be sure of retaining the vitality of your work.

**1** Draw a grid directly onto the surface of the image or onto a sheet of tracing paper or thin acetate laid over it. Use marker pen if using acetate.

**2** Draw a larger grid with the same number of squares but to the same scale as on your drawing paper.

**3** Copy the contents of each square on to the equivalent square on the drawing paper. Plot the main points where shapes or edges cross over the perimeter of each square into the next one, carefully, before developing the detail.

# Masking

A mask is anything that protects the surface of your drawing and prevents colour from being applied to a specific area. The simplest form of mask is a piece of paper laid on to your drawing paper; the pencil can travel up to or over the edge of the paper and when you lift the mask, the colour area has a clean, straight edge. You can obtain hard edges using cut paper; torn paper makes a softer edge quality. You can also use thin cardboard, or pre-cut plastic templates such as stencils and French curves.

If it is important to mask off a specific shape or outline, which may be irregular or intricate, you can use a low-tack transparent masking film which adheres to the paper while you work, but lifts cleanly afterwards without tearing the surface. You lay a sheet of masking film over the whole image area and cut out the required shape with a craft knife. Carefully handled, the blade does not mark the paper beneath. Low-tack masking tape can also be used to outline shapes; it is available in a choice of widths, and the narrower ones are very flexible for masking curves.

## Loose masking

Thin cut or torn paper can be used as a mask either to protect your work from smudging, or to keep an area clear of colour while working right up to the edge, without the need for a linear outline.

**1** Place the paper mask on the drawing paper and hold it down firmly. Begin by shading lightly over the edges of the mask.

**2** Build up the shaded colour to the required density, keeping the direction of the pencil marks consistent at each side of the mask.

**3** Lift the top corner of the mask to check that you have a clean edge quality and the right intensity of colour. Keep the lower edge of the mask in place, so you can just drop it back if you need to rework the colour area.

# Using masking tape

Masking tape will give a straight edge to create a clean 'frame' around a drawing, avoiding the need for a ruler. A hard edge might be used for a geometric structure, or it can be stretched slightly or cut to mask curves.

**1** Lay down the masking tape evenly, but do not rub too firmly, or you may have trouble lifting it without damaging the paper surface. Shade colour over the edges of the tape as you would with paper masks. An advantage of masking tape is that you can work over both sides of the tape at once. When complete, peel back the tape carefully.

**2** If you are overlaying colours, you can use the same mask, or a fresh piece of tape, to cover the paper while you lay the second colour.

# Using masking film

This is useful for hard-edge, precise work, especially where an image is to be repeated. It has the advantage of being slightly sticky so that it will stay in place while you shade in the cut-out shapes. Practise cutting the stencil with a craft knife, as curves are not always easy to cut accurately.

**1** Trace the outline of your drawing on paper. Detach the top edge of the masking film from its backing sheet and smooth it down on the paper covering the image area with a border of film all around. Gradually pull back the rest of the backing sheet, smoothing the film across the paper as you go.

**2** Identify the first shapes you are going to colour, and cut around them with a sharp craft knife. Lift one corner of the cut film and peel back the shape. Repeat as necessary. Apply the coloured pencil to each shape filling it with colour up to and over the masked edges.

**3** When you have completed all areas in one colour, move on to the next. Cut and lift the mask sections in sequence, then shade in colour.

**4** At this stage the colouring is complete, and the uncut masking film is still on the paper, causing the black background to look greyish. The next stage is to remove the remaining masking film completely.

**5** Compare the finished effect to step 4. With the mask removed, the edges of the coloured areas stand out sharply against the black, making each shape clean and distinct.

# Erasing techniques

An eraser can be used both to make corrections and as a drawing tool, although in both cases the process works slightly less well than with graphite pencils. Even so, lightweight strokes are easily eradicated, and in many cases, alterations can be made to regain a surface suitable for reworking. As a drawing tool, use your eraser to create lighter or negative marks on a darker surface, although this will not be effective on washed areas.

The type of eraser you choose will depend on your paper: a kneadable eraser for smooth papers and something firmer, such as a plastic eraser, for more textured ones. Try both and see which you prefer. You can cut a plastic eraser to a suitable size for more precise work, such as the soft feathered edge of animal fur, and kneadable erasers can be pulled into a point. Densely compacted colour can be scraped back with a craft knife to open it up a little or to allow for further work with an eraser.

**Eraser alterations**
*The pencil work had become heavy and too dark on the wine glass. An eraser is used to take out some of the excess pigment.*

**Making alterations with a knife**
*Similarly, a sharp blade used with care removes pigment that has become too heavy and allows light into the picture.*

### Eraser drawing

For Cat in the Garden, *the artist has used an eraser as a drawing tool to lighten the leaves in the foreground and to lose the definition of the trellis at the right-hand side.*

### Softening blends

The Pavilion at Marston *shows subtle layering and integral use of an eraser to soften the colour blends and to lighten it in places, notably patches of sky and in the foreground.*

# Rectifying mistakes

Marks made with water-soluble pencils can be removed by simply wetting them with water and lifting off the resultant 'paint' with a rag or kitchen paper. Repeat several times, as long as you are working on stretched paper (see page 16), and leave to dry thoroughly before reworking. This is often the most effective way to remove unsuccessful drawing. Rather than working too precisely, it is often best to take out a wider area around the problem, leaving a soft or ragged edge, or to work up to a hard edge which might form a natural break in the drawing, so that the new drawing blends in seamlessly. Alternatively, a cotton bud can be used for precision.

White gouache or acrylic could be used to conceal unwanted marks, so long as the surface is busy enough for you to integrate the change in texture.

**ARTIST'S TIP**
Subsequent layers of pencil and wash on an acrylic underpainting will not muddy it, as acrylic is resistant to water. Colour can be wiped away to reveal the clear colour underneath, perfect for rectifying mistakes.

## Searching for perfection

Alteration to preliminary work can often be a bonus, adding texture and depth – or history – to the finished piece. In the search for the perfect line or descriptive mark, reshaping, or even removing can be part of the drawing process. Leave the 'wrong' one in until you are sure of the right one to avoid making the same mistake twice. Or leave it in as part of the drawing; the eye will always pick out a true line from previous permutations.

*Exploring structure*
*This is the initial stage of the later drawing shown on page 71. The drawing in red explores the structure, and the angle of this metal goat has been allowed to tell its story, and indeed plays an important part in conveying a sense of liveliness to this static object.*

# Making alterations

Alterations are easily disguised if the paper surface is undamaged. Enough pigment can be removed for further work even if the paper is discoloured. If the subsequent drawing is to be lighter, a little white paint can be dabbed over to provide a more neutral ground colour. This sequence shows you how to implement alteration techniques effectively.

**1** The barn on the horizon in this landscape is to be moved slightly to the left. The new position is sketched in and a rag dampened with water is used to gently wipe away most of the unwanted drawing. The drawing is removed around the area to be changed, softening the edge.

**2** When the paper is completely dry, the barn is redrawn and the surrounding area blended into the new work.

**3** The new position of the barn makes for a more satisfactory composition.

# Underpainting

To underpaint, either lay an all-over ground colour before you start, as shown on page 45, using thin acrylic paint, watercolour or even thin oil or oil pastel, or use the paint as the first stage in the drawing, blocking in the main shapes of your composition, and choosing colours that will play a role in the colour relationships of the finished piece.

If you decide on the latter approach, remember that because coloured pencils are less opaque than paint, the base layer will affect the covering layer and darken it, so use a lighter shade on top to combat this. Your choice of colour depends upon those to be applied later, but in general, choose a base colour that will enrich the final layers. For example, you could use a harmonious burnt sienna or warm yellow under a red for a light, bright effect, or you might establish the main light and dark passages in muted monochrome tones, a cool blue or warm grey.

## Underpainting with primer

A primer stops the paper absorbing pigment, and can be used in a considered way to alter the surface texture before painting. The bright white of an acrylic primer can add brightness to translucent or thin layers painted or washed over it, and the dry primer will reveal brush marks which can be integrated within the surface texture, contrasting with any unprimed areas.

**1** Underpainting with acrylic primer produces an interesting textured surface to work on with water-soluble pencils. Use a bristle brush and coat the paper with primer straight from the pot. When dry, the brush marks will remain slightly raised, providing a texture that plays an integral role in the look of your finished piece.

**2** When colours are shaded over the primer, the brushmarks will show to give a hatched effect.

**3** Water is added using a soft brush and brushed over the waterproof surface. The wet pigment flows over and into the crevices.

## Underpainting with acrylic paint

Ordinary acrylic paint in white or a colour is less textural than acylic primer, but will act as a barrier between the paper and subsequent work. Remember: The chosen hue of the paint will affect the colours used however, as shown in the example here.

*Here the same two colours are shaded over a yellow ground and water is then added. You will notice the yellow pigment alters their colour and how they blend to form a neutral brown with yellow overtones.*

### Underpainting with toning colours

*This hot landscape was underpainted in acrylic in a bright turquoise blue for the sea, sky and island section and a rich burnt sienna for the foreground. Although all the underpainting is well covered, it still influences the overlaid colour, adding a sense of light and brightness.*

### Underpainting with contrasting colours

*In comparison, the same landscape was underpainted in a cool complementary blue-grey which gives the completed picture a slightly muted feel, although there are flickers of interest where the blue is allowed to show through, and to contrast with the reds and oranges.*

### Monochrome underpainting

East Coast Beach Huts *was begun with a monochrome pencil underpainting, using reds of different tonal value blended with water. Only light pressure was used, just enough to indicate the changes in tone before continuing in full colour.*

# Mixed media

Coloured pencils can be a useful addition to other media, adding texture as well as being used to define or clarify a drawing previously worked in pastel or paint. You might try a few different methods, such as working with coloured pencil over blended oil pastel, drawing into a coloured-paper collage, making a line and wash drawing with a fibre-tipped pen and water-soluble pencils or combining watercolour.

## Oily surfaces

Thin oil paint or oil pastel spread with a little mineral spirit makes a pleasant fluid surface to draw on. The grease seems to mix with the pencil pigment and intensifies the colour although it can leave a stain, especially on coloured paper, so use only where it will be camouflaged by further work.

## Building up in more than one medium

Thin acrylic, gouache, watercolour and coloured inks can all be used in conjunction with pencils to build up the image as well as for underpainting. Colour the drawing with water-soluble coloured pencils using shading or hatching, and blend with water. Or draw with a combination of coloured pencils and one of the several types of pastel available – all contribute varying qualities of colour and texture.

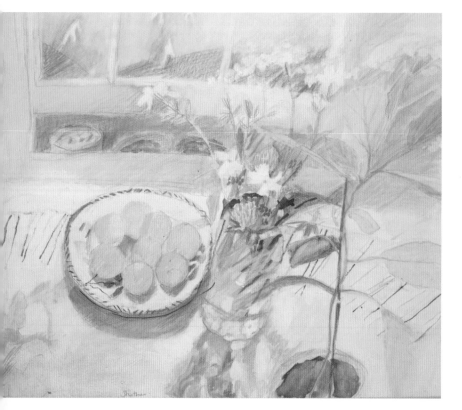

***Variety and contrast***
*In* Cricket and Wildflowers *the contrast of the drawn lines and the brushed ones give variety and liveliness. Coloured inks, white gouache and water-soluble pencils are thinly laid, with the white textured ground playing a major role in conveying the airy freshness of the subject matter.*

◀ **Line work** *Both coloured pencil and graphite lines have been used in* Table at the Window, *and although minimal, they play an important role, emphasising geometry and perspective in an otherwise soft-focus oil pastel rendering.*

▼ **Line and wash** *In the pages from a sketchbook shown here, fibre-tipped pens of different thicknesses were used for the drawings, which were then coloured using wet and dry pencil. Further detail was added after the paper had dried.*

# CHAPTER 3

# Colour

# All about colour

All colours have three distinctive properties that account for their appearance: hue, tonal value and saturation. Manufacturers tend to use descriptive and somewhat subjective names for their colours, one may describe a green as 'grass green', while another will describe a similar hue as 'spring green'. In a large box of pencils, you will find many different hues, and many different tones of each one, usually more than you will need, and certainly more than you would wish to carry around. It is therefore important to understand how these characteristics interact and the relative effect of colour so that you can select a few to work with at a time.

### Relative tonal value
*A grey scale made from 'cool' unmixed greys sits alongside unmixed reds, yellows and blues, demonstrating their relative tonal value. The nature of yellow changes as it becomes darker, whereas the reds and blues retain their identity.*

## Colour terms

**Hue:** Simply another word for colour, referring to the generally accepted colour name of an object – grass green, daffodil yellow, poppy red. This may be more specifically described in certain light conditions as yellow green or even as spring green or emerald, further differentiating the hue from other greens.

**Tonal value:** The relative lightness or darkness of a colour. Some colours are intrinsically darker than others; lemon yellow is light in tone while indigo is naturally dark.

**Saturation or intensity:** Refers to how bright a colour is. Prismatic colours are fully saturated, while subdued or muted colours are less vivid and may be referred to as chromatic greys.

# Hue, tonal value and saturation

Yellows, blues and reds of differing hue, tonal value and saturation are grouped together below to show the range within just one colour name. The yellows show the least tonal change as yellow quickly loses its identity as it becomes darker, but they all demonstrate wide ranges in hue (where the colour is placed on the colour circle) and saturation (how bright or how dull they are).

**Blues** *These are easily classified whether they vary in hue from those on the green side of the spectrum, to those juxtaposed with the violet. Tonal variation and purity have little effect on their blueness.*

**Yellows** *If you place the lightest yellow and the darkest against the grey scale on the previous page, you can gauge the fairly narrow breadth of tone compared to that of the lightest and darkest reds and blues.*

## ARTIST'S TIP

Try grouping your pencils as 'reds', 'blues', etc. and in doing so you'll become familiar with the range of hues within a group and the variations in tone and intensity.

**Reds** *These cover the spectrum from red violet through orange and are often not seen as 'red' at all, but described as pink, brown or terracotta.*

# Prismatic colours

Prismatic is the term used for the pure colours in the spectrum, the primary and secondary colours as seen in a rainbow: red, orange, yellow, green, blue, indigo and violet. Three of these are primary colours, which cannot be made by mixing other colours together. The primaries are red, blue and yellow when dealing with pigment, and red, blue and green when dealing with light.

This difference is becoming more familiar through the increased use of home computers for colour printing. The screen image is in RGB (red, green and blue), but the images are printed out using inks in CMYK (cyan, magenta, yellow and black).

Secondary colours are two primaries mixed together; for example, red and yellow make orange. However, no pigment represents a true primary colour, as pigments don't behave like colours of light. Instead they tend to have a bias towards one or other of the colours that is next to them on the spectrum. The purest orange will be made from a red and a yellow with a bias towards one or the other, but a whole range of oranges can be made from any number of combinations of reds and yellows.

## Mixing primary colours

By combining the primary colours, a number of secondary hues can be obtained. Below are just some examples of the variations that can be achieved through mixing.

*Yellow and red are mixed together to form orange (top row). In the second row, yellow ochre and terracotta form a brownish orange, while in the third a light, greenish yellow and a cool pink combine to form a peachy orange.*

*Blue and red In the top row, these are mixed to form a dark brownish violet; in the second row they produce a warm red violet and in the bottom row the light, cool violet and dull pink mix to form a silvery grey.*

*Blues and yellows Many shades of green can be obtained by mixing blues and yellows. Here they vary from an olive green (top of the second column) through to a rich grass-green (bottom of the second column).*

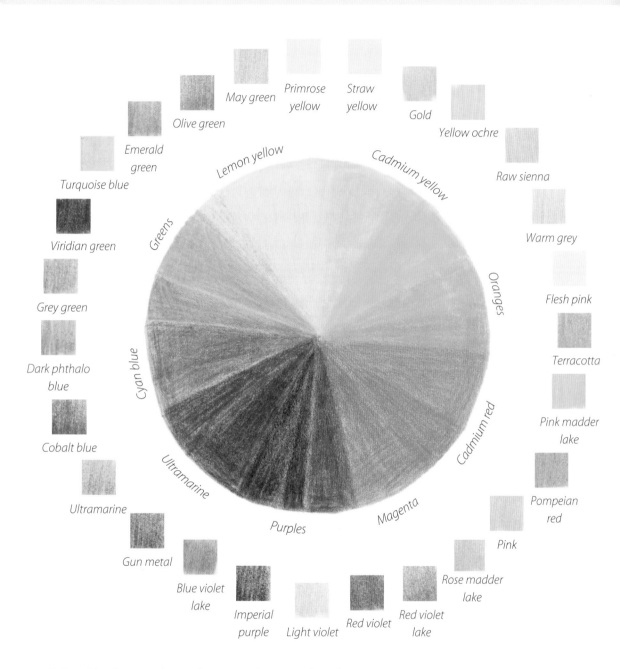

May green

Primrose yellow

Straw yellow

Gold

Olive green

Yellow ochre

Emerald green

Lemon yellow

Cadmium yellow

Raw sienna

Turquoise blue

Greens

Oranges

Warm grey

Viridian green

Flesh pink

Grey green

Cyan blue

Cadmium red

Terracotta

Dark phthalo blue

Pink madder lake

Cobalt blue

Ultramarine

Pompeian red

Ultramarine

Purples

Magenta

Pink

Gun metal

Blue violet lake

Imperial purple

Light violet

Red violet

Red violet lake

Rose madder lake

**Colour bias** *Pigments have a bias towards one or other of the adjoining colours of the spectrum. In this colour circle (the spectrum joined up) coloured pencils from several different brands are grouped to show their colour bias.*

# Warm and cool colours

Colours are often described as warm or cool, but this is a relative term. It's generally understood that, on the colour circle, the green, blue and violet range are the cool colours, while the red, orange and yellow range are the warm ones. But within these categories, every colour has varying degrees of warmth and coolness. For example, magenta, although a red, has a definite blue bias, so is described as a cool red, while vermilion has an orange bias and so is considered to be a warm red.

▾ *Warm palette*
*Cliff at Newgale is worked up from fibre-tipped pen on-the-spot sketches, as a preliminary to a much larger painting. The palette is mostly warm and colours are muted, with contrast found in the relative tonal values.*

## Warm and cool primaries

Red and yellow are often described as warm colours, and blue as cool, although there are variations in temperature within each hue. The crimson reds have a blue bias, and are cooler than the more orangey reds, such as cadmium red, while an orangey yellow, such as cadmium yellow, is warmer than the acid lemon yellow. Some blues are purplish, veer towards red, and are therefore warmer than those with a greenish tinge, such as turquoise. Below, three primary colours are shown with the warm version on top and the cooler below.

**Warm**

Cadmium red     Cadmium yellow     Ultramarine blue

**Cool**

Crimson Lake     Lemon yellow     Cerulean blue

**Cool palette**
*Predominantly cool colours from the crimson to yellow-green part of the spectrum are used in* Green Moon and the Goat, *apart from a very small dash of yellow ochre on the extreme left.*

## ARTIST'S TIP

If you have a large set of pencils you will find it helpful to line them up in a warm to cool continuum. This will help you sort out the bias of any one colour (see page 67). You may find the difference in tonal value confusing at first, but you will soon begin to see whether a so-called neutral colour in fact leans towards yellow, blue or red.

# Complementary colours

Complementary colours are those that are opposite one another on the colour circle. There are three pairs of these colours: red and green, yellow and mauve and blue and orange. In their purest state they don't contain any of each other, so provide the greatest contrast when placed side by side. They play an important role in working with colour, as they have the effect of enhancing each other.

If you look at paintings in any media you will often see how artists have used these contrasts, bringing mauves into shadows on a yellow object, for example, or using touches of red among greens of foliage.

Complementary colours are also very useful for 'knocking back' a colour that is too bright, as they become less saturated and less contrasted if overlaid or blended together. A red, for example, could be muted with a light overlay of green. If mixed or overlaid in equal proportions, the identity of each colour will be almost lost, producing what is known as a chromatic grey.

## Harmonious colours

Any two or three colours that lie next to each other on the colour circle will appear harmonious – because they share a common base colour, they work well together without jarring. A picture painted predominantly in harmonious colours would be described as having a narrow hue range, and would convey a sense of quietness or calm. Even if prismatic hues, fully saturated red and orange are chosen, the colours are less gaudy than they might be if used in conjunction with similarly saturated complementary turquoise or emerald green.

**Harmonious and complementary**
*An harmonious range, in this case a slightly greenish lemon yellow to turquoise, would sit quietly together; but the study is dominated by the addition of the cool blue, which changes the dynamics and sets up a complementary relationship with the lemon yellow.*

**Strong harmony**
*In this study the harmonious element of the colour scheme is stronger than the one shown on the left, as both extremes contain blue. This time the complementary contrast, between either the emerald green and dark red-violet or the light grey-violet, is more subtle.*

### Complementary colours in use

In Goat Nudging Jug, *the strong complementary blue heightens the vivid reds and oranges. Further contrast is generated by mixing these two complementaries together, as seen in the integrated shading of the background strip behind the pears. The lime green of the pear and the red-violet immediately around it set up an echoing diversity.*

### Subtle complementary effects

*The complementary contrasts in* Cacti, *although evident, are less vivid than in* Goat Nudging Jug *above (the salmon pink with the olive green, and the yellow ochre and raw umber with the grey-violet). The colours appear less intense, partly because of the influence of the green-grey paper, and partly because the palette includes a number of less saturated or intense colours, in places dulled down by mixing complementaries. These can be seen in the greens and reds of the cactus on the right and in the dark patches in and around the flowerpots.*

# Colour and mood

Colour is not only a means of describing what we see – it can also be used expressively to convey a mood or atmosphere. Bright or light colours – known as 'high key' – tend to evoke a happy response, whereas dark-toned colours such as browns, deep blues and purples – 'low key'– give a sense of stability and thoughtfulness.

Using harmonious colours, which are those next to one another on the colour wheel, create a gentler, more restful atmosphere than strongly contrasting colours such as complementaries (see page 70) or vivid primary colours. In landscape, colours tend to be harmonious – greens, yellows and blues – indeed you may sometimes need to exaggerate or even invent a contrasting colour to avoid dullness. Flower and still-life painters often deliberately set up groups consisting mainly of harmonious colours such as pinks and mauves, with perhaps a touch of a muted complementary or a lighter tone for contrast.

*Terracotta*

*Raw sienna*

*Olive green*

*Blue grey*

*Yellow ochre*

*Imperial purple*

*French grey*

*Flesh pink*

**High-key palette**
A Corner of Green *by Laura Duis, uses a high-key but muted palette, with strong tonal contrasts. The composition is carefully organised, with the light areas established from the beginning.*

Scarlet

Cyan or
Spectrum blue

Ultramarine

Dark violet

Cool grey

Turquoise green

Lemon yellow

### Low-key palette

Formal Gardens at Hidcote *is relatively low in key and conveys
an atmosphere of an impending summer storm. The palette is
limited, consisting largely of scarlet, dark violet, ultramarine,
cyan blue, turquoise green, lemon yellow, white and cool grey.
Scarlet and lemon yellow were blended with water and used for
the initial underpainting, followed by several layers of the mainly
prismatic colours to suggest dark shadows. Highlights were
emphasised by erasing and then redrawing in lemon yellow.*

# Lightening and darkening colours

The pressure you use obviously affects the lightness or darkness of the colours, but you can also mix colours on the paper surface to change the tones, even laying light colours over dark (if using water-soluble pencils, you can lighten colours simply by adding water). Although coloured pencils are most often worked from light to dark, as they are semi-transparent, white is relatively opaque, as are many of the lighter colours, because they have a higher proportion of white in their make-up than the dark colours. Interesting effects can be achieved by working pale pinks over browns, or pale yellows over greens. When darkening colours, try to avoid too much use of black; this can have a deadening effect. The examples shown on the opposite page will give you some ideas.

**ARTIST'S TIP**
Vibrant 'darks' are evoked by often surprising mixtures of bright reds, oranges, dark blues, greens, violets; or these can be added to brown or black. The depth of tone will be far greater than that achieved with just a black even with heavy pressure.

***Lightening and darkening in context***
*Garden at Chengdu Museum is confined to mainly prismatic greens, yellows, blues and reds in coloured pencil and inks, blended with water and overlaid with loose hatching. Some of the light patches have been further lightened with gouache and spattered with bleach, which removed some of the ink. The screen on the left was begun with a pink ink wash and knocked back with pencil work in warm browns, purples and ultramarine, blended in some places with water. The shadows of the foliage are darkened using ultramarine and some whites and yellows are included. The paper is firm with a fine grain enabling an effective build-up of layers.*

Scarlet lightened with white (left) and darkened with ultramarine (right).

Grass green lightened with lemon yellow (left) and darkened with ultramarine (right).

Lemon yellow lightened with white (left) and with added grass green (right).

Ultramarine lightened with grass green (left) and darkened with burnt umber (right).

Burnt sienna lightened with flesh pink (left) and darkened with ultramarine (right).

Violet lightened with water (left) and darkened with umber (right).

Persimmon pink ink darkened with violet (left) and knocked back with burnt sienna (right).

# Overlaying colours

The majority of coloured-pencil renderings depend upon the effects of overlaying colours. In this way you can achieve richness of hue, tonal density and contrast, and effective three-dimensional modelling of forms and surface textures. Because coloured-pencil marks have a degree of translucency, with applications being influenced by the paper colour or other colours beneath, the process of building up a drawing in layers creates potential for many subtle variations of hue, shade and texture.

There are many different ways of overlaying colours: you can put one layer of shading over another to modify colours and produce interesting mixtures and gradations; you can build up a network of lines, dashes and dots to develop complex effects of optical mixing; or you can enliven areas of flat colour by overlaying a linear pattern or broken texture that subtly meshes with the original hue.

Colour layering provides greater depth and detail in a drawing: you can achieve active colour qualities in highlight areas or dark shadows, which intensify effects of light and atmosphere. In a practical sense, overlaying colours is equivalent to mixing paints in a palette: if you don't have the precise hue that you need, you can create it from a blend of two or more colours.

## Overlaying water-soluble pencils

**1** A pink water-soluble pencil was used for the initial line drawing, to merge quietly with subsequent drawing. Shading in lemon yellow was added and blended with the pink using a wet brush. Highlights were dabbed out with a rag while the colour was still wet.

**2** Loosely hatched blue pencil describes the form of the dish, and was worked into the shadows. Further loose hatching in black and Prussian blue was used to fill in the 'negative' shapes around the dish, the scribbled marks echoing those used for the grapes. Some of the pencil work was merged with water to denote the darker shadows, and more delicately, to produce the pale grey around the grapes in the centre.

**3** The fluid patterning in the foreground was made by painting water shapes, filling in with a pencil to make a soft pigmented pool, and then pushing the colour about with the brush. This was lightened in some areas by lifting out with a rag and added to with pencil and water. Once dry, more pencil work was layered over the top to give a veiled appearance.

**4** The grapes were developed with several layers of wet and dry pencil. Loose shading and line drawing reveal the colour beneath. Water was used to soften blends, taking care not to lose the linear work altogether, however, the shapes of the grapes are described as much by the drawing of the surrounding shadows, as by these linear marks.

**5** *The Blue Dish*
*Layering need not result in dense compacted colour. Here, open shading and loose watercolour washes are combined with free line drawing.*

**ARTIST'S TIP**
As you begin to learn how colours work together, experiment with overlaying using a very small palette of six colours; two yellows, two reds and two blues, choosing a warm and cool version of each.

CHAPTER 4

# Planning and Procedures

# Choosing a viewpoint

If you are working from life rather than from sketches or photographs, the first stage in composing your picture is to decide on your angle of viewing. It is surprising how radically even raising or lowering your own eye level can affect a scene, so try looking at it from both a seated and a standing position – in landscape, a low viewpoint will make more of the foreground, and high one will emphasise the distance. You may also find that a slight shift from one side to another may make a big difference. For example, a group of trees might overlap and thus be hard to read from one angle, but if you move to the right or left they will separate out.

In still life, a high viewpoint will often yield a more dramatic composition than the more common eye-level one, as it organises the object into a pattern. Try setting up your group on a low table, or even on the floor, and work standing up.

## Using a viewfinder

Very few artists are without one of these simple devices. A viewfinder consists of nothing more than a piece of card with a rectangular aperture in the middle, and can be made in minutes. By holding the viewfinder up at various distances from your eye, you can bring the subject close or push it away, and so decide how much to include, and whether cropping would help the composition. You can also work out the best format by holding it up first horizontally and then vertically.

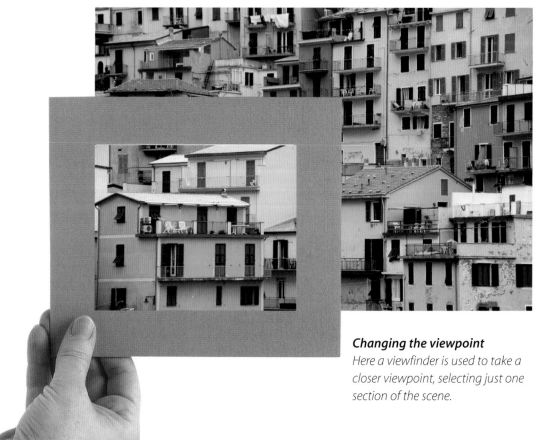

***Changing the viewpoint***
*Here a viewfinder is used to take a closer viewpoint, selecting just one section of the scene.*

### Changing the emphasis

The viewpoint shown in photo *A* is perfectly satisfactory; it makes a good composition, as the diagonals of the roof and walls lead in to the more distant buildings. However, you might consider changing the emphasis by focusing in more closely on the foreground building to give a more geometric structure to the image (see photo *B*). Use the viewfinder to explore possibilities.

### Exploiting shape and texture

In photo *C*, the photographer has aimed at contrasting the strong shape of the cactus with the distant mountains and the diagonals of the clouds, but you could explore the shapes and textures by taking a closer viewpoint and letting the cactus fill the whole of the picture (see photo *D*). In this case, it would be best to omit any distracting background detail.

# Choosing a format

Once you have decided on your viewpoint, the next stage is to decide on the format of your drawing – whether you want to work on a horizontal rectangle (landscape format) or an upright one (portrait format). Sometimes this will be obvious, but it isn't always, so use your viewfinder again (see page 80) to frame the subject in different ways. If you are working from a photograph, cut two L-shaped pieces of card and move them around on the photo – there is always a temptation to use the same format as the photo, but you may find that by taking a section from the middle of, say, a landscape, you can make a more exciting composition, using an upright shape.

## Paper formats

Drawing papers are made in standard-sized rectangles, but you don't have to stick to these proportions – you might prefer a very long rectangle, or even a square, in which case you simply leave some of the paper uncovered. If you do this, it is best to sketch in lines where you intend the drawing to begin and end, otherwise you will be inhibited by the edges of the paper.

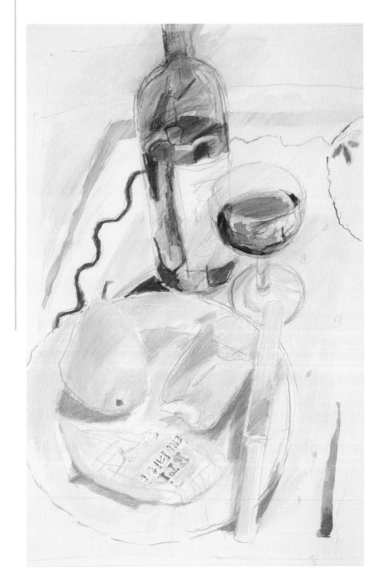

**Elongated rectangle**
*In this piece, an unusually tall portrait format has been chosen to accomodate the long diagonals of the knife and table edge. Commissioned for a book cover, the illustration is allowed to bleed freely at the edges.*

**Landscape format**
*In* Street Cleaner, *the classic landscape format makes use of strategically placed horizontals and verticals. It is loosely drawn in coloured pencil and inks spattered with bleach, which reinforces its light, airy quality.*

**Square format**
The Pink House *almost fills the frame, determining its shape. Acrylic and oil pastel have been used boldly in blocks of colour, the linear marks of the coloured pencil work tying them together in the initial drawing, and also adding texture and movement.*

# Composition

There are few hard and fast rules about how to design or compose, a picture, but you should aim for a good balance of shapes and colours so that you create a harmonious whole rather than a series of unrelated elements. To make links between different parts of the image, a common device is to create 'echoes', by repeating similar colours and/or shapes from one area to another. In a landscape with a blue sky, you might bring in touches of blue among the greens of grass, and balance a foreground tree with a similarly shaped one in the middle distance.

It is vital to keep the viewer's interest, so don't leave large areas where 'nothing is happening', and if there is a dominant feature, avoid placing it too centrally; symmetry tends to split the image into two halves, leaving no centre of interest. Don't divide a landscape into equal areas of land and sky – a good ratio would be two thirds to one third of either sky or land. Try also to lead the eye into and around the picture by means of visual signposts. In landscape, curves, or diagonals, which the eye naturally follows, can be used to lead into a focal point – these could take the form of a path or fence running in from the foreground to the middle distance. In still life, folds of drapery can be used to perform the same function.

## Making compositional choices

Below is a sequence of sketches made before deciding on a final composition for the finished piece. The objects are moved around, before a horizon line is decided upon.

**1** In this asymmetrical composition, the horizon line is just above the halfway mark, with most of the detail in the bottom half. The objects are carefully spaced. The eye is drawn diagonally up and to the right of the horizon line to the tall jug, and the two half shapes form a connection by taking your eye from one side and to the other, but not out of the picture.

**2** This is far less interesting. It is too heavy at the left-hand side and the eye is drawn along the horizon but has nowhere to go but back again.

**3** This lacks cohesion, as the line at the top doesn't relate to the table top below, but the space could be given distance using directional marks and the layering of colour.

**4** This tonal study makes a rough pattern of the light and darks. Almost square in format, the four large objects are used to fill the space, with only one of them seen 'whole'.

**5** The final plan looks at the light sources more carefully. Some of the objects are changed or moved to create a feeling of greater distance and suggestions for colour have been included using a limited palette of three or four hues.

**6** In the finished piece, slight changes have been made. The juxtaposition of the objects is reinforced and the way the light falls is clarified. While preliminary sketches can help with compositional choices, it's not always necessary to keep exactly to the plan!

# Sketching

Coloured pencils are an excellent medium for sketching – clean, lightweight, easily portable and versatile. You can work rapidly in line only to describe individual shapes and forms, or build up colour masses quickly, with loose shading and hatching. Select at least one pencil from each of the main prismatic colours (see page 66) and perhaps a couple of extras, such as an ochre or olive green or cool grey (see Basic palette, page 19), although you will find that for really quick sketching, two or three held ready in your other hand for instant changeover may be enough.

If you already know your subject and thus have some idea of its colour range, you can choose pencil colours accordingly – greens and blues for some landscapes, and reds and browns for others, for example, but remember that you will need the complementaries to your main selection for contrast and nuance (see page 70).

**Analysis** *Pencil sketches analysing difficult perspective or detail are useful to take back to the studio. Here, the relative sizes of the chimneys and the lighthouse is important, as is the perspective and the detail of the lantern.*

**Line drawings** *A fibre-tipped pen is handy for simple line drawings. Here the focus is composition, so only the main shapes are extrapolated, and coloured pencil is then used to record local colour and relative tonal value.*

## ARTIST'S TIP

If you intend to make sketches on which to base a finished work, you will need more visual information than if you are simply sketching for its own sake. So if you don't have enough time – or the right colours – to give a full account of the scene, make written notes in the margin of your sketch. And if the weather is changeable, it is also a good idea to carry a camera to record the scene as it was when you began the sketch.

***Recording the main elements*** *This quick sketch shows the lighthouse in situ. It is simply drawn with little extraneous detail, but care has been taken to record the relative proportions of the buildings and the main differences in light and shade.*

## THE TRAVELLING KIT

If you are out on a sketching trip there are several tools you should consider taking with you. A graphite pencil and an eraser may prove useful, as might a fine-line fibre-tipped pen for quick sketches. You may wish to work on large sheets of paper rather than a sketchbook, in which case a drawing board will be essential – a folding easel is also a great asset. Aside from these extras, essentially, for a day out you will need:

• Basic palette of coloured pencils (see page 19)

• Sketchbook (your favourite size, shape and orientation)

• Bulldog clip or clothes peg to hold the pages open

• Watercolour brush

• Screw-top plastic pot for water

• Paper towels

• Craft knife for sharpening

• Plastic bag or something waterproof to sit on

# Drawing styles: Loose

Loose drawing styles will vary between artists, but as a general rule, the whole image is worked on simultaneously, with a gradual build-up to the completed piece. This way of working allows for changes in composition, perspective or scale to be made easily, as a feeling for the whole image can be seen from the start. Changes can be either disguised or incorporated into the work, and you won't encounter the problem of finding that you have spent hours working on one section only to find that it is too big or too small.

The work can be defined or refined as you wish; the stages in modelling form, enhancing light and shade or developing detail can be halted or continued at virtually any stage.

**1** An initial drawing is made in a warm ochre pencil using a strong, definite approach. The colour will easily blend in to the subsequent drawing and will not inhibit any future changes.

**2** Light shading is added in blue and overlaid with red in more shadowy areas. The loose hatching creates a sense of liveliness; the red and blue together suggest a deep warm darkness appropriate to the subject.

**3** This close-up shows work in the heavily shaded areas; loose hatching and crosshatching are employed to gradually build the density required.

**4** Shading is blended with water, deepening the colour and tone and providing a smooth surface on which to layer further colour when dry.

**5** Shading and hatching using dry pencil in dark blue is overlaid; but the grainy texture of the paper now impregnated with red still shows through.

**6** New colours are added and yellow ochre is applied to the jar, and then wiped over with a damp paper towel to soften and blend the drawn marks.

**7** The layered area of dark tone behind the onion is sufficiently compacted to allow sgraffito to be used effectively to denote the fine dried roots.

**8** The round tomatoes and their shiny skin gradually evolve through a combination of drawing and blending with a brush. The highlights are removed with an eraser on dry paper.

**9** Loose, heavy shading partially blended with water in yellow ochre and blue-violet conveys the fairly rough texture of the table top and chopping board. Continuing in the same free manner, details are added to develop form, such as the deeper tone under the potatoes and around the tomatoes.

**10** Greater contrast is needed in other areas, and here an indigo pencil is used to help the background recede and so give depth to the jar. However, as the shadows recede, more light (in the form of the red underpainting) is allowed to show through.

▶ *Jane Strother*
Stone Jar with Vegetables
*The finished picture is both strong and lively, helped by the method of working over the whole picture at once. Surprisingly few colours have been used. Taken from across the spectrum but tending to be warmer variants, predominantly the red-blues – ultramarine, violet and indigo – yellow ochre, scarlet and French grey.*

# Drawing styles: Tight

Working in a 'tight' or controlled manner suggests a methodical way of working from a careful initial drawing through to completion, with little room for changes to be made during the process. Adaptations can be made however, so long as the paper texture isn't altered by too much rubbing out.

In this demonstration, sections are completed separately before moving onto the next, from left to right, as the artist is right handed, to reduce the possibility of smudging.

**1** The initial drawing is transferred to the drawing paper using tracing paper, working in line only with a sharp HB pencil and light pressure. The artist concentrates on the detailed parts of the composition.

**2** This close-up shows part of the flower area transferred to the drawing paper using graphite pencil. Small blobs of reusable adhesive putty can be used to blot the surface. This prevents the grey graphite discolouring subsequent coloured-pencil work.

**3** The brickwork and the archway are lightly coloured in to judge the effect, avoiding any heavy pressure which could fill the paper grain.

**4** Once the colours are established, layers are built up to achieve the desired effect, with careful modelling of form by observation of shadows and highlights.

**5** A battery-operated electric eraser easily removes small circles representing the flowerheads without damaging the paper or disturbing the surrounding work.

**6** The flowerheads are carefully added in yellow coloured pencil, and the surrounding detail is developed using a brown pencil.

**Robin Borrett**
Abbey Gardens

*In developing this work,
the artist has concentrated on
the texture of the background
trees, slowly increasing the
detail as he moves towards
the foreground. A relatively
small palette has been used –
depth of colour and breadth
of hue have been achieved by
layering. An electric eraser or
blob of reusable adhesive
putty easily lifts off colour
where alterations are
necessary. Gradually the
whole surface is covered and
painstakingly finished to the
same level of detail.*

# Comparing methods: Loose

Here, two artists using differing approaches have reworked the same photograph, *Poppy Fields*, (shown right) in coloured pencil. As in the examples on pages 88–101 the obvious point of departure is in the initial drawing. In the loose style, Artist A keeps to the same level of development for the whole picture at all times and uses a greater range of gestural marks whereas Artist B's tight style is very even in its surface quality. Greater use has been made of the effects of colour contrast in Artist A's piece, resulting in greater vibrancy and suggested mood.

***Poppy Fields*** *The original photo with its brightly-coloured poppies and contrasting blue sky is interpreted by each artist in their own individual way.*

**1** After making a very loose sketch to 'place' the hillside and the field, the poppies are indicated in red acrylic paint without any further drawing. The paint ensures their redness, as any underlying colour would affect the purity of the red.

**2** With the poppies in place, the composition is mapped out with a light blue-grey pencil. Blues are lightly hatched to indicate the sky and shaded areas.

**3** The overall view shows a colour indication for the whole picture area. Even though the shading is very light, at this stage, it is still important for the marks to follow the form of the hillside, and the direction of the grasses.

4 Blending the shading with water removes most of the 'white' areas, although the colour is still very translucent. The red poppies are kept free of stray brushwork, but the rest is freely worked.

5 The background is worked up in blue, green, grey, and violet, still following the contours and defining the shape of the group of buildings.

**6** Continued work on the hillside creates richer colour, and the paper grain remains evident through the layering. Some of the drawing describing the monastery needs changing and is easily removed with a damp rag.

**7** Redrawing is left for the moment while the field is developed to the same level as the hillside, with heavier use of yellow and light greens, and some red shading towards the back.

**8** A compass point used as an impressing tool over previously coloured greens and yellows, is tried as an experiment, to evoke the waving barley in the foreground. The lighter marks are subtly revealed when overlaid with a different shade of green.

**9** The poppy shapes are strengthened with reds and indigo centres, using a pencil occasionally dipped in water. Further drawing in olive green defines the stalks and grasses in the foreground.

**10** A bright warm yellow shaded over the greens ties whole areas of the field together, its translucent quality allows the layering underneath to show through.

**Jane Strother**
The Monastery
*In the completed picture the grain of the paper
is evident in the shading of the hills, giving an
appropriate mottled texture, and contrasting
with the more linear textures in the foreground.
The buildings are redrawn, with care taken to
keep the roofs light and bright. There is no
white paper showing; the 'white' patches are
lightly covered during one of the initial washes
and with a white pencil (in the sky).*

# Comparing methods: Tight

Artist B uses a much tighter style in his recreation of the same photograph. The concentrated approach implemented here results in an intricately worked drawing. Artist B takes time to build up his work section by section, producing an evenly worked, detailed piece, although the colour contrasts are much less evident than those displayed in Artist A's interpretation of the same subject.

**Poppy Fields** *The same photograph is reworked by Artist B in a much more detailed and methodical way than Artist A's style.*

**1** Working lightly the artist begins with the foreground after transferring the initial sketch to drawing paper using tracing paper. The main shapes are accurately drawn from the beginning.

**2** The flowerheads, stalks and grasses of one section are completed before moving on, working from left to right and from front to back. White paper is allowed to show through the hatching. A sharp pencil point is crucial for this degree of detail.

**3** After working up the stalks with a green pencil using varied pressure, spaces for more flowerheads are erased using an electric eraser, which takes out exactly the required amount of colour.

**5** The hillside is built up, slowly and painstakingly copying the texture and colours. The pressure is still light, and hence the white grain of the paper remains, the depth of tone created by layering.

**4** In this example, the artist works from front to back, from the field to the undergrowth, and then to the hillside. His more usual approach is to work from left to right, which keeps his hand away from the finished work.

**6** The sky begins to complete the picture. The overall feel is of calm and light due to the even pressure and paper grain, which helps to unify the surface.

**Robin Borrett**
Poppy Field
*In the final stages, the poppies are given more
definition, and a few stalks and heads of wheat added,
but care is taken not to overwork the foreground, as this
would detract from the focal point of the picture.*

# CHAPTER 5

# Themed Palettes

# Buildings

The appearance of buildings is dramatically affected by the light that falls on them. Strong shadows and bright light will define the geometry, the scale and the detail, all of which will be softer, sometimes even hidden, with lower light level. The character of a building can be revealed by your choice of colour and contrast, as well as your use of mark-making or composition.

### Pure colours

1 Straw yellow
2 Rose pink
3 Sky blue
4 Spectrum blue
5 Ultramarine
6 French grey
7 White

### Colour mixes

8 = 1 + 2
9 = 2 + 1
10 = 1 + 2 + 3
11 = 4 + 5
12 = 4 + 1
13 = 6 + 1
14 = 4 + 7

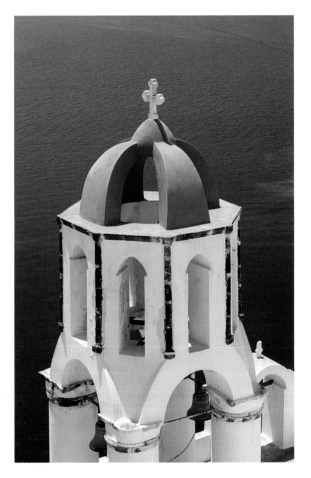

**Chapel by the sea** *A lovely building like this, shining white in the sun against a deep blue sea, asks to be painted – but is it really white? It is easy to misjudge how light the building actually is; in a black-and-white photo the shaded and sunlit pillars would be very similar in tone to the roof. You will need to choose a colour to represent white, in this case, muted light pink, and yellow, sky blue and cool light grey could be tried.*

**Pure colours**

1 Gold
2 French grey
3 Cold grey
4 Light violet
5 Rose pink
6 White
7 Light warm grey

**Colour mixes**

8 = 1 + 4 + 5
9 = 2 + 4 + 6
10 = 1 + 7 + 4 + 6
11 = 6 + 7
12 = 4 + 3
13 = 1 + 2
14 = 3 + 6

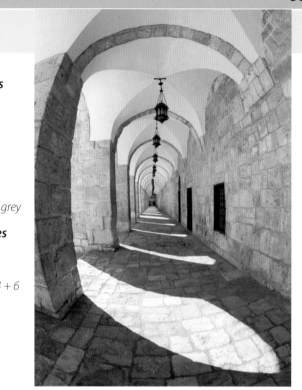

**Cloisters** *Muted colours, low in saturation are needed here; the interest should be developed by the observation of perspective and tonal contrast, darks being achieved by layering rather than using ready-made, dark colours.*

**Pure colours**

1 Ochre
2 French grey
3 Raw umber
4 Pomperian red
5 Hookers green
6 Turquoise green

**Colour mixes**

7 = 3 + 6
8 = 4 + 3
9 = 4 + 2
10 = 6 + 2 + white
11 = 6 + white
12 = 6 + 1 + white
13 = 5 + 4
14 = 1 + 6

**The mine** *Two photos have been layered to convey an aged and melancholic feel symbolic of a past industrial landscape. Mixed media can be employed effectively here, a tea bag or sponged coffee used as a ground and then worked on when totally dry with dense pencil hatching in browns, oranges and olive green.*

# Landscapes

For landscape work you can start with the basic palette suggested on page 19 and add further colours depending on whether your landscape is, for example, green and wet or hot and dry. To depict rainy or misty days you will need less tonal contrast and gentler colour than for full sunlight, which in turn will alter according to whether the sun is overhead or lower in the sky. When the shadows are shortest, in the middle of the day, colour is often bleached out, while when the sun is low, colours appear richer and more saturated.

### Pure colours

*1 Ochre*
*2 May green*
*3 Orange*
*4 Olive green*
*5 Prussian blue*
*6 Ultramarine*
*7 Dark violet*

### Colour mixes

*8 = 6 + white*
*9 = 7 + 4*
*10 = 1 + 2*
*11 = 3 + 1 + 2*
*12 = 7 + 6 + white*
*13 = 6 + white*

**Mountain landscape** *Complementary contrasts between the ultramarine blue of the lake and the golden ochre of the sunlit hillside, are on the blue side of the spectrum, the warm ochre being muted by a green undertone in many places. Keeping to one side of the colour circle in a painting (there is an absence of obvious red in this image) can give it an overall feeling of calm. To obtain the dark contrast, however, you may need to include a hidden complementary in your mix.*

**Pure colours**

1 Turquoise green
2 Phthalo blue
3 Olive green
4 Blue violet
5 French grey
6 Warm pink
7 Lemon yellow

**Colour mixes**

8 = 7 + 1
9 = 7 + 1 + 2
10 = 3 + 1
11 = 3 + 2
12 = 4 + 2
13 = 7 + 3
14 = 3 + 5
15 = 6 + 5
16 = 4 + 6
17 = 4 + 7 + 6

**Morning light in the forest** *Your palette will need a cool bias to represent the soft muted colour in this image. The canopy is blue-green in colour, the olive-green-grey trunks can be worked in lemon yellow on the sunlit side, and there are blue-violet shadows on the light-brown leaf cover.*

**Pure colours**

1 French grey
2 Blue violet
3 Orange
4 Straw yellow
5 Cadmium yellow
6 Warm pink
7 Phthalo blue
8 Ultramarine

**Colour mixes**

9 = 1 + 3
10 = 5 + 3
11 = 5 + 6
12 = 6 + 4
13 = 6 + 2
14 = 2 + 1
15 = 3 + 8
16 = 8 + white
17 = 7 + 1 + white

**Sunset, Lake Powell** *The only real tonal contrast in this photo is between the darkest shadows in the centre and the brightest rocks. Generally the colours are tonally similar and rely on subtle contrasts of high-key colour. You will need a palette of light yellow-oranges, pinks and violets, and for the shadows a light phthalo blue and a warm French grey with some dark blue.*

# Portraits

To select a palette for a portrait you will need to observe the sitter in context, as skin colours are much affected by the surroundings and light conditions. For instance, a face with a pale skin tone, lit by a table lamp and the light reflected from a warm red curtain, will look quite different to the same face outdoors on a cold winter's day. You may, of course, choose to place the subject against the light so that the face is in shadow and both the colours and features less distinctive.

### Pure colours
*1 Sepia*
*2 Ultramarine*

### Colour mixes
*3 = Mixes of 1 + 2 with*
*varying degrees of pressure.*
*4 = 3 + white*

**The girls** *Working from a monochrome photo gives you the opportunity to concentrate solely on tonal differences. You may like to try working with two colours, a warm brown and a cool blue for a greater density in the shadows.*

**Pure colours**
1 Light violet
2 Cold grey
3 Sepia
4 Rose pink
5 Ochre
6 Cobalt blue
7 Pompeian red

**Colour mixes**
8 = 5 + 1
9 = 5 + 2 + 4
10 = 5 + 1 + 2
11 = 7 + 1
12 = 7 + 6

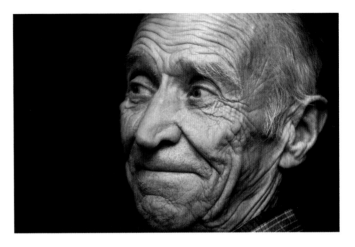

**The old man** *The bright light shows up the man's wrinkles that give his face such character. Unify the picture with blues and browns, orange and ochre, and maybe a little violet; the background needs to be dark and densely layered, and the same colours used to describe the expressive lines on his face. The lighter skin colouring could be added afterwards almost as a veil, and burnished in places to create a shine.*

**Pure colours**
1 Ochre
2 Sepia
3 Pompeian red
4 Rose pink
5 Cold grey
6 Olive green
7 White
8 Ultramarine

**Colour mixes**
9 = 1 + 4 + 2
10 = 1 + 4 + 2 + 7
11 = 6 + 4 + 7
12 = 6 + 7
13 = 6 + 8
14 = 6 + 5
15 = 2 + 4 + 7
16 = 2 + 7

**At the window** *The features on the left almost disintegrate into the shadows, enhancing their delicacy. For these, use warm browns, yellows and ochre and some Prussian blue and crimson to complement, both when darkening the tone and for building up clothing and flower detail.*

# Skies

Skies can play a major, even predominant role in a landscape composition by their sheer scale; the feeling of 'big space' can be controlled by altering the horizon or contrasting colour or tone. Bad weather often brings dramatic cloud formations, dark with rain while a shaft of sunlight lights up a ribbon of land. On a bright, windy day, high, fast-moving clouds cause shadows to scud across the land altering the tones and the intensity of colour from one moment to the next.

### Pure colours

1 Phthalo blue
2 Cobalt blue
3 Hookers green
4 French grey
5 Gold
6 Rose pink
7 Pompeian red

### Colour mixes

8 = 6 + 5
9 = 6 + 5 + 1
10 = 1 + white
11 = 2 + white
12 = 2 + 1
13 = 4 + 1
14 = 5 + 4 + 1
15 = 5 + 4
16 = 3 + 1
17 = 7 + 3 + 2

**Misty morning** *The distinction between sky and water is hazy, though emphasised by the clouds' reflections. Use the same cool blue-grey for the water and the haze in the sky, deepen and darken it in the foreground in response to the lighter clear blue at the top left. The golden reflection is a near complementary to the colour of the water, with the greatest contrast at the right-hand side. Overlay dark blue or green and red-brown for the trees until you find the depth of colour you need, rather than using black.*

**Pure colours**

1 French grey
2 Blue violet
3 Phthalo blue
4 Prussian blue
5 Viridian green
6 Cadmium red
7 Warm pink
8 Lemon yellow

**Colour mixes**

9 = 3 + white
10 = 3 + 1 + white
11 = 1 + white
12 = 2 + 7
13 = 8 + 7 + 1
14 = 8 + 5
15 = 4 + 5 + 3
16 = 6 + 3
17 = 4 + 6

**Wind** *For this image, proportion is important, the sky occupies four-fifths of the picture space. The focal point, the almost silhouetted figure, is the darkest element, and you would need to reduce the intensity of the red shirt with Prussian blue, black or viridian green, or a mixture of all three. Notice how the sky, although lighter, varies in tone across the horizon and is not a clear blue, and that the grasses and other foliage appear indistinct in the low light level.*

**Pure colours**

1 Ochre
2 Smalt blue
3 Ultramarine
4 Azure blue
5 Cobalt blue
6 Indigo
7 French grey
8 Emerald green

**Colour mixes**

9 = 2 + 7 + white
10 = 3 + white
11 = 2 + white
12 = 5 + white
13 = 6 + 4
14 = 8 + 6
15 = 8 + 2 + white
16 = 7 + white
17 = 1 + 7

**Rain approaching** *These storm clouds form a deep, dark band just below the halfway line, echoed by the finer, dark blue-green band at the horizon. Try a range of blues and green, layered over each other to create muted hues, and complement with a similarly muted French grey and raw sienna beach.*

# Still life and flowers

Still life subjects for drawing or painting are most often groups of objects chosen and strategically placed by the artist, but suitable subjects can sometimes be found in situ, for example pebbles on a beach or objects in a greenhouse or garden shed. There is such a wide range of possible subjects that the choice of colours must obviously depend on your own interests.

### Pure colours

*1 Light ultramarine*
*2 Magenta*
*3 Scarlet*
*4 Lemon yellow*
*5 Viridian green*
*6 Cyan blue*

### Colour mixes

*7 = 1 + 2*
*8 = 2 + 3*
*9 = 2 + 3 + 5*
*10 = 5 + 4*
*11 = 4 + 1*

**Tulips** *The pinks and greens in this image will appear clear and bright if worked on bright white paper, beginning with flat shapes, and adding darker tones after an initial blocking in. The vivid contrasts are best obtained from the complementary colour contrast of the pinks and greens, and the differences in tonal value.*

## Pure colours

1 Orange
2 Cadmium yellow
3 Olive green
4 Emerald green
5 Prussian blue
6 Cyan blue
7 Light blue
8 Apple green

## Colour mixes

9 = 2 + 1
10 = 2 + 1 + 3
11 = 1 + 3
12 = 1 + 3 + 4
13 = 4 + 6
14 = 7 + 8
15 = 2 + 8
16 = 2 + 5
17 = 1 + 5

**Beach pebbles** *A large set of pencils may include a number of light (L) and dark (D), cool (C) and warm (W) greys or browns, which will be useful for attempting a group of pebbles like these. Include your basic palette too, though, and lightly shaded and layered complementaries will also produce colourful greys, the layering adding texture to your drawing.*

## Pure colours

1 May green
2 Turquoise green
3 Lemon yellow
4 French grey
5 Warm pink
6 Raw umber
7 Dark violet

## Colour mixes

8 = 2 + 3
9 = 2 + 1 + 3
10 = 1 + 2
11 = 4 + 2
12 = 6 + 1
13 = 5 + 6
14 = 5 + 6 + 1
15 = 6 + 7 + 1

**Morning tea** *The teacup and newspaper, although subtly lit and with some tonal variation, is really a study in warm, high-key hues. Select a range of warm pinks and browns, an ochre, warm and cool greys and a blue before you start. Plan out your composition and shade the main shapes lightly with flat colour to cover the paper surface before developing form and detail.*

# Trees and Foliage

Not only does leaf colour change through the year, but the appearance of tree trunks or branches will depend on weather conditions and the variety of the tree. Looking up into the canopy, the leaves will often appear dark against the sky. Colour permutations are more or less infinite, so try to bring variety into the greens and browns.

### Pure colours

1 Cadmium yellow
2 Naples yellow
3 Lemon yellow
4 Orange
5 Apple green
6 Cobalt blue
7 Dark violet

### Colour mixes

8 = 2 + 5
9 = 2 + 3
10 = 1 + 3
11 = 1 + 3 + 4
12 = 4 + 3 + 6
13 = 1 + 4
14 = 2 + 7
15 = 1 + 6

**Autumn leaves** *To maximise the light on the yellow leaves, the glimmer of white light should be kept to a minimum or the yellow will appear too dark in contrast. The yellow can be enhanced by using a purple bias for the almost black branches, and by mixing a little blue with the dull green in the background. The red-orange hue on the right works well with the tonally similar olive greens.*

**Pure colours**

1 Orange
2 Cadmium yellow
3 Olive green
4 Emerald green
5 Prussian blue
6 Cyan blue
7 Light blue
8 Apple green

**Colour mixes**

9 = 2 + 1
10 = 2 + 1 + 3
11 = 1 + 3
12 = 1 + 3 + 4
13 = 4 + 6
14 = 7 + 8
15 = 2 + 8
16 = 2 + 5
17 = 1 + 5

**River bank in Autumn** A limited palette of two or three greens, a couple of blues and an orange or two is enough to represent this vibrant composition. Much of the foliage apart from the lime greens, can be layered with an orange underpainting to unify the composition. Overlay this with olive green and grass green and ultramarine for the very dark areas.

**Pure colours**

1 May green
2 Turquoise green
3 Lemon yellow
4 French grey
5 Warm pink
6 Raw umber
7 Dark violet

**Colour mixes**

8 = 2 + 3
9 = 2 + 1 + 3
10 = 1 + 2
11 = 4 + 2
12 = 6 + 1
13 = 5 + 6
14 = 5 + 6 + 1
15 = 6 + 7 + 1

**Avenue** Cool light green foliage and green-grey trunks could be set off by contrasting with a warm pink complementary as an underpainting or mixed with raw umber for the leaf litter and darker areas. Make the most of a greater tonal contrast on the left and right with more lemon yellow in the foliage and the addition of dark violet on the trunks.

# Water

An expanse of still water seen at a distance presents a mirror-like surface that will take on the colour of the sky, but because water is transparent, when seen close to it will become the colour of the lake or river bed, and will also be affected by the colour of any substance dissolved in it or carried by it. So your palette can be chosen from an infinite number of colours. Start with the suggested basic palette and add specific hues according to your subject.

### Pure colours
*1 Warm pink*
*2 Ochre*
*3 Phthalo blue*
*4 Sky blue*
*5 Ultramarine*

### Colour mixes
*6 = 2 + 1*
*7 = 2 + 5*
*8 = 3 + 5*
*9 = 3 + 2 + 5*
*10 = 4 + 3*

***The pool*** *The rippled reflections in this outdoor pool would be difficult to draw from life, but the photograph freezes the fluid shapes, allowing you to extrapolate a pattern to develop in quite a small range of colours. Observation is the key, once you have explored the shapes revealed in photos, you should find it easier to paint directly from your subject.*

**Pure colours**

1 White
2 Turquoise blue
3 Ultramarine
4 Dark violet
5 Raw sienna
6 Cold grey
7 Hookers green
8 Orange

**Colour mixes**

9 = 1 + 2
10 = 1 + 2 + 5
11 = 6 + 2
12 = 6 + 2 + 3
13 = 4 + 3
14 = 4 + 6 + 7
15 = 8 + 5 + 7
16 = 8 + 5

**High tide** *Bright whites need to be seen in relation to the tonal value of the colours surrounding them. In this image the white spray is the focal point and needs to be enhanced by strong contrast with the hues and tones of the sea. Even the foam is surprisingly dark, so use dark blue-greens and cool browns for the sea, with creamy white and warm light grey for the spray.*

**Pure colours**

1 Ochre
2 Turquoise green
3 Emerald green
4 Dark violet
5 Red violet
6 Hookers green

**Colour mixes**

7 = 1 + 2
8 = 2 + 3
9 = 6 + 3
10 = 4 + 3
11 = 4 + 6
12 = 5 + 2

**Shallows** *This study in green can be represented by close observation of the fluid shapes and patterns, and the changes in tone. Use blue-greens and a little yellow ochre with a complementary red or red-violet to enhance the darker patches of the scene.*

# CHAPTER 6

# Gallery

# Landscape and seascape

**The Wave**
by K. Scott McGregor
*Working mainly with water-soluble pencils,
and using layering and blending techniques,
the artist has given a wonderfully accurate
account of the breaking wave and the
plumes of spray. The picture is full of life and
movement due to the use of repeated curves
and strong tonal contrasts.*

### Morning Surf, Monhegan Island
by Kendra Bidwell Ferreira
*By focusing in closely on a small section of the rocks and water, the artist has produced a wonderful patterned effect reminiscent of a lacy fabric. Minimal layering of colour has been used – the white foam and waves are areas of the paper which were sketched in and have been left white. The colour is juxtaposed and mixed by the viewer's eye and the strong tonal contrasts enhance the delicate fragility of the swirling water.*

### Perpetual
by Jeff George
*In this atmospheric work, dry coloured pencils have been used more as a painting than a drawing medium; careful, painstaking layering and blending have ensured that no pencil marks are visible. The artist has worked on blue paper to give an overall cool blue cast to the painting, and to avoid the reserved highlights on the rocks from appearing too bright.*

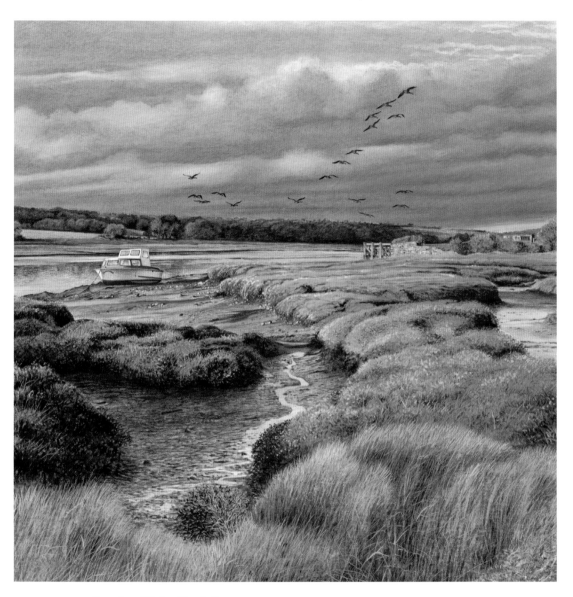

**Evening Flight, Hook Quay**
by Graham Brace
*This scene was worked in the studio from notes, observations and
photographs. It was begun with a coloured ground laid with pastel pencils
rubbed and blended into the surface and then fixed, and continued with two
different brands of dry coloured pencils, one softer and waxier than the other.
The fine detail in the vegetation was achieved by scratching out, together
with some fine brushwork in gouache paint.*

## Equanimity
by Susan L. Brooks
*The artist has chosen to work on sanded paper designed for pastel work, which grips the pigment very firmly and allows for a considerable build-up of colours. The colour scheme is a simple but highly dramatic one, based on the yellow/violet complementary contrast.*

## Riparian Winter
by Richard McDaniel
*An unusually wide, shallow landscape format has been chosen for this image to make the most of the lovely sweep of the river running from foreground to middle distance. The tones and colours have been built up by several layers of hatching and crosshatching, but blending has been kept to a minimum in order for the pencil marks to play a part in the composition.*

### Mountain Landscape
by Mark Hudson
*The painting was begun with light washes of watercolour to form the ground (this is still visible in the immediate foreground). Rough shading and hatching with coloured pencils contribute to the atmospherics of the sky, while linear work in the foreground suggests the textures of the grass. The colours chosen are natural hues that both reflect the subject and create a harmonious mood.*

**A View Near Biggin Hill**
by John Townend
*The style used here is bold and free. A strong sense of rhythm and movement is achieved through bold outlines defining individual forms together with multi-directional hatching and crosshatching, especially noticeable in the foreground.*

**Forest Light**
by Mike Pease
*In this piece, tonal contrasts are used to create the strong light effect. Simultaneously, the muted background colours and small, intricate shapes, give a misty, fragile quality to the rendering.*

### *Stone Summerhouse – Belvoir Castle*
by Robin Borrett

*The textures play a major part in this picture. The three main areas of grass, stone wall and flowers each have a specific texture. The early layers were kept light, and bolder and darker colours were added to create form. Scratching out the pigment and impressing techniques were used in the area at the top of the steps to accurately render the form of the twigs and branches in the shrubbery.*

**Reflections of Venice**
by Vera Curnow
*The artist has used an interesting technique for this rendering. Working on illustration board, she covered the whole surface with low-tack adhesive film, cutting and peeling it away section by section as she worked with wax-based coloured pencils and mineral spirits. In the final stages, detail was added with dry pencils.*

# Nature

***The Palm Jungle***
by Dyanne Locati
*For this powerful image, which has strong
abstract-pattern qualities, the artist has used even
shading to build up the shapes and forms and
achieve subtle variations of tone and colour. The
grain of the paper allows the applied colours to
'breathe', adding sparkle to the rendering.*

**Tulips**
by Angela Morgan
*The complex arrangement of petals and leaves
that forms this composition is created with a faint
pencil outline. Although the overall effect is light
and fresh, the pencil colours have been laid with
a confident, free technique. The orange tulips are
a vibrant blend of yellow, orange and red pencils,
and the more delicate pinks are similarly
described with varying tones of the basic hue.*

**Butterfly**
by Kendra Bidwell Ferreira
*When depicting small-scale objects such as these, accuracy is essential; an impressionistic approach would not convey the essence of the subject. The butterfly has been very carefully drawn, as have the flowerheads, and built up in layers to achieve depth of colour and tone. Notice that the flowers at the top have been treated in less detail, while those just behind the butterfly are in sharp focus.*

### Buffy the Cat

by Richard Childs

*This is one of a number of studies of this cat, and here the artist has focused closely on the face, creating a highly dramatic and eye-catching composition. The whiskers were achieved by impressing lines with an inkless ballpoint pen and then working many layers of soft coloured pencil on top.*

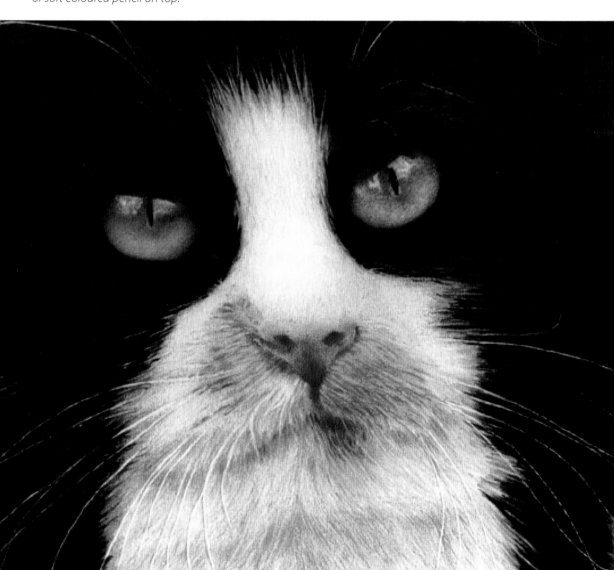

**Spectrum**
by Vera Curnow
*Both the red/green complementary contrast and tonal
counterchange have been exploited here, with an excellent
balance of light, dark and middle tones. Notice especially
the pattern made by the 'negative shapes' behind the buds
and stems on the left. The artist has used wax-based
coloured pencils blended with mineral spirits, and has
given the work a glossy finish by applying thick fixative.*

**Nina's Rose**
by John Hayes
*This piece was drawn from an enlarged photograph, using
a light box. The darkest tones were added first using small
overlapping circular strokes, decreasing the pressure towards
the lightest area of each tone. A colourless blending pencil was
used to blend the coloured layers in the same circular motion.
Further blending was undertaken with a paper stump (torchon)
dipped in solvent. This eradicated any coloured-pencil lines,
before a layer of white was added and rubbed gently with a
paper towel, helping to create the carefully placed highlights.
A black gouache background and light layer of fixative
sharpens the finished picture.*

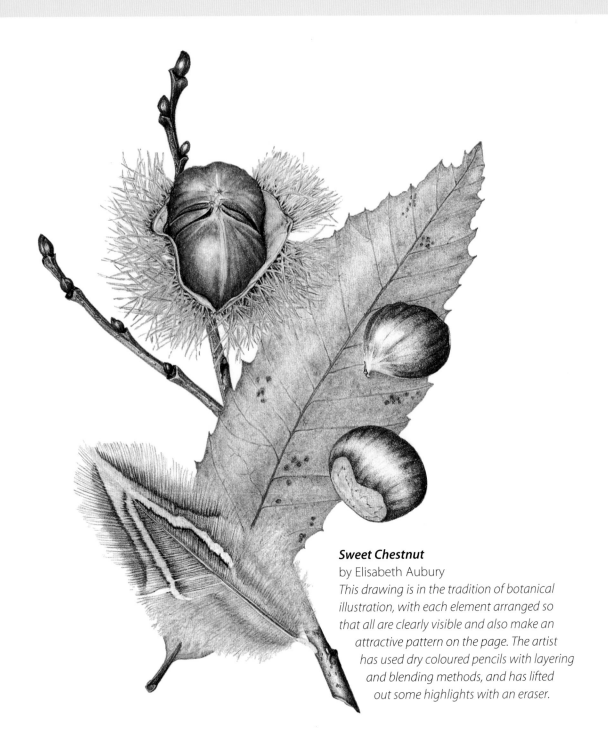

**Sweet Chestnut**
by Elisabeth Aubury
This drawing is in the tradition of botanical
illustration, with each element arranged so
that all are clearly visible and also make an
attractive pattern on the page. The artist
has used dry coloured pencils with layering
and blending methods, and has lifted
out some highlights with an eraser.

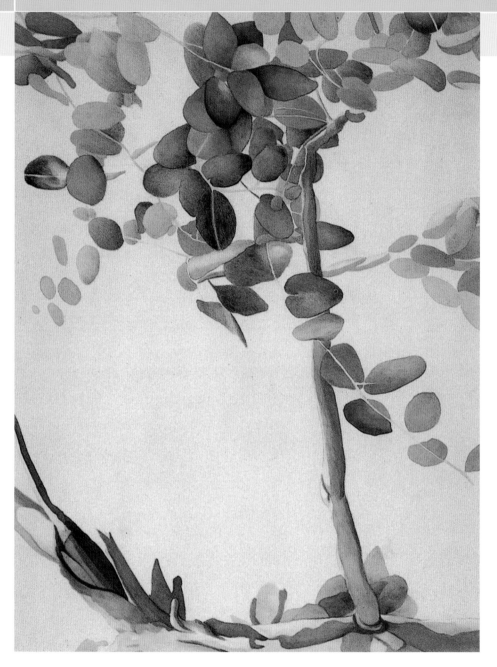

**Eucalyptus** by Steve Taylor
*The leaf shapes in this piece are simple forms, and so a controlled tonal balance is essential to the complexity of the rendering. The artist has chosen gentle watercolour hues which have been strengthened with light pencil shading. Paper has been left bare or very lightly painted where veins and stems show white against the colour.*

### Roses and Apples

*by Robert Maddison*

*This drawing addresses a traditional still life subject, but the elements and arrangement are challenging. Intense colours and reflective surfaces are paired with complex patterns and shapes. Here, the artist has focused on the subjects' abstract qualities to emphasise the contrasts in the composition.*

### Fox in Autumn

by Steve Taylor

*Most of the modelling and atmospheric description is created here with watercolour, subtly modified with water-soluble pencils. The movement is expressed by the fluid lines of the fox – the angle of its body and the downward thrust of the head, as well as the more obvious motion of its legs and paws.*

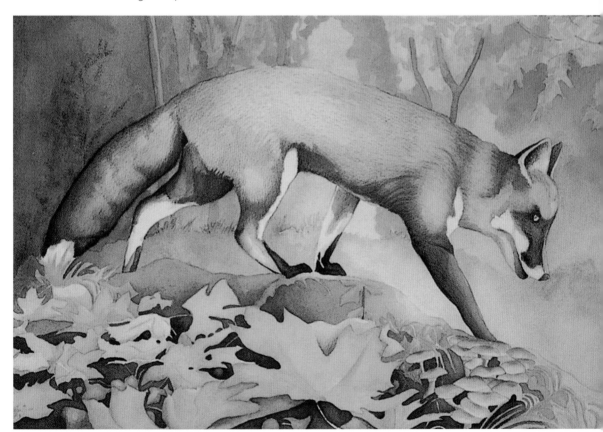

### Border Collie

by Richard Lovesey

*In this lovely drawing, the artist has captured both the texture of the hair and the expression of the dog – it is very much a portrait of a specific animal rather than just a dog.*

**Hope of Sepilok**
by Richard Childs
*This wonderful drawing was inspired by a
visit to the orangutan sanctuary in North
Borneo, and was done from a photograph.
The texture of the animal's fur was built up
with many layers of soft coloured pencil,
which were then burnished with hard strokes
of a colourless blender in the direction of the
fur. White, cream and French greys were then
laid on top for the wispy hairs.*

### Bad Language
by Robin Borrett
*This picture illustrates how coloured pencils work so well when illustrating animals. Using a fine point, the artist has created the animal's coat with accurate detail. The bridle was treated differently by burnishing, creating a smoother surface without showing the pencil strokes.*

### The Merry-Go-Round
by Angela Cater
*For the artist, this was very much a nostalgic piece, as she spent many happy times on the merry-go-round with her Grandmother. Dry coloured pencils were used to build the colour in layers, working from light to dark. The detail on the saddles was impressed into the paper using an empty ballpoint pen, so the white paper was then retained when colour was overlaid.*

# Still life

**Sweet cherries**
by Kendra Bidwell Ferreira
*This piece was begun with a wash of indigo blue coloured pencil and solvent for the plate. Light red coloured pencil and solvent were then used as an underpainting for some areas of the cherries.*

*Beginning with a wash helps to eliminate some of the texture of the paper, although white paper was left to create the carefully-placed highlights on the cherries. Layers of dry pencil were then added for depth of tone and to deepen the contrast with the plate.*

### Pears

by Kendra Bidwell Ferreira
*The artist has organised both the objects and the lighting to ensure that cast shadows play an important role in this image. Notice how the contrast between warm and cool colours is used to build up the forms, rather than relying on tone.*

### Bowl with Apples

by Peter Woof
*This is an interesting example of cropping to make a more powerful composition. The central area of the plate, with the strong pattern framed by the sweeping curve, provides the perfect background for the gently coloured, rounded forms of the apples. The artist has used soft, waxy coloured pencils, which facilitate blending, and has worked on heavy watercolour paper.*

**Death Row**
by Jeff George
*This piece was completed section by section: the woodgrain perimeter first, followed by the interior of the matchbox, then the colourful match-heads, the matchsticks and finally the box exterior. In each segment the darker layers were added first, before working towards the lighter values.*

### Empty Nest

by Jeff George

*Empty Nest has been worked on a black illustration board. The door is composed of three different layers of white coloured pencil, a hard lead white pencil to establish the local colour of the door, a slightly softer, more opaque white pencil to enhance and enrich the details, and then a final layer of soft pencil to achieve the brightest highlights. Blues and lavenders were then layered on top to give tints of colour, and to increase contrast and drama, a black pencil was used to develop small shadow details.*

# Portraits

**Self Portrait**
by John Townend
*The strong contrasts of black and red, together with the complementary contrasts of green shadow areas, creates a powerful, almost aggressive effect. The mood is emphasised by the busy pencils marks, weaving over and around each other to describe form and texture.*

**Portrait of Caith**
by Katriona Chapman
*The mood of this portrait is serene
and gentle, as befits the subject. The
artist has used watercolour pencils on
board, skillfully blending to achieve
soft gradations of tone and colour.*

# CHAPTER 7

# Subjects

# Landscapes

**Beach with palm tree** *This subject demands a painterly approach, using water-soluble pencils or blending with solvent for the background and beach. Use a clear, light turquoise green and raw sienna together with more muted colours such as greys and blue-violet. The tree can be described with more linear marks.*

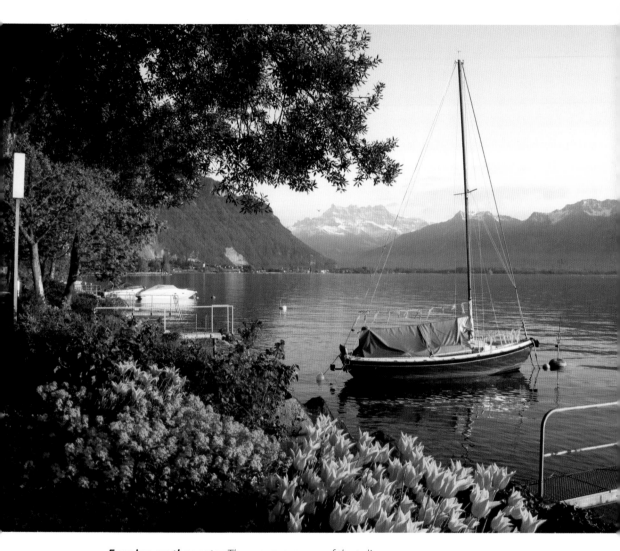

**Evening on the water** *The warm oranges of the tulips in the foreground can be echoed subtly throughout the picture area, hinting at the warmth of the evening light bathing the promontory in the middle distance, the trees and the water. Warm pinks and ochres will modify and unify the greens and blues, allowing the pure cobalt blue of the boat to stand out in contrast.*

**Autumn colours** *Underpainting in lemon yellow would unify the colours in this composition, enhancing the bright orange and making a good ground colour for the trees. Keep the yellow clean and fresh, and build up the foliage with small strokes of well-sharpened pencils to create a stippled effect, layering dark colours over light. If necessary small patches of light can be revealed with sgraffito.*

**Desert** *Blending two complementaries gradually reduces the intensity of each. To begin, copy this image in cyan blue and red-orange, varying the pressure. Add yellow for the highlights and perhaps burnt sienna, but keep your palette to a minimum.*

**Lakeside** *The lakeside is mirrored almost perfectly. Use tracing or transfer paper to transfer the image. Once the colours have been built up to a compacted surface, burnishing or work with an eraser will help you achieve the blurred effect in the water. For the clouds, you might try mixing white gouache with a little wet colour rather than leaving the paper white. The intense blue should be built up by layering dense colour, working on a bright white paper for the best results.*

**The Beck** *The translucency of water is not easy to achieve. Start with the underlying colours – the browns, yellows and greys – and once the surface is compacted, burnish with white or a selection of pale tints. Very thin acrylic, mixed with a medium rather than water, could be applied with a brush or a sponge, but it shouldn't become too wet. Work quickly, as the wet paint will 'melt' the pencil marks, making the mixture difficult to control.*

# Nature

**Poppy** The calyx and the stamens probably need to be worked up first from a carefully observed drawing in order to keep the image crisp. Use well-sharpened pencils for this area to provide a contrast with the softer petals, which could be worked with blended water-soluble pencils and added linear work for the tonal detail.

**White flower with bee** *You will need no more than a handful of pencils to tackle the flower. Work on a smooth-surfaced paper which will allow white and pale tints to show up, and describe the overlapping petals by building up the tones in layers. Use a sharp pencil at all times to keep the work fresh and achieve the sharp edge quality. Experiment with blues and violet combinations for the greatest resonance in the background area.*

**Conkers** *This close up shows off the exciting textures of the shiny conkers, their prickly cases and the veining of the leaves. Make the most of this in your work by burnishing compacted layers of reds, burnt sienna and dark blue for the markings, and experiment with sgraffito or impressing for the leaf veins, using different implements for the various thickness of line.*

**Olives** *Notice the part the soft, out of focus background plays in this simple but powerful image, contrasting with the sharp clarity of the olives and a very subtle use of complementary colour. Use just a handful of pencils to begin with: olive green, of course, plus a more yellow-green, burnt sienna and a dark and light violet.*

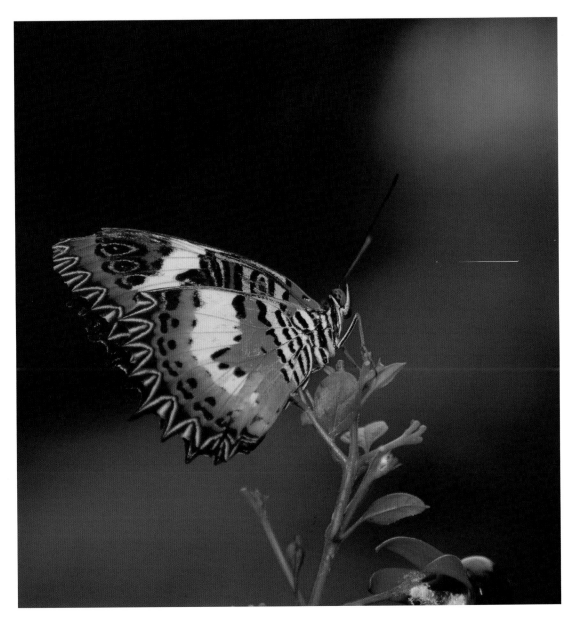

**Butterfly** *The strength of this photographic image is in the contrast between the small but vibrant colour and patterning of the butterfly and the soft, dark, out of focus background. In order to accentuate this differentiation you could work on stretched white paper and mask out the image carefully with masking fluid until you have painted the background, or alternatively you could work on dark coloured paper, keeping the image distinct with well-sharpened pencils.*

**Seashells** *Shells are not easy to draw, as the spirals and the general asymmetry require close observation. Contour drawing is perhaps the best way to attempt this – describe the volume in terms of fine lines of differing weights, in two or three colours.*

# Animals

**Kitten in close-up**
For animal fur, blend by a combination of shading and light hatching. Use a plastic eraser in the direction of the fur to soften the blends and blur the edges. Shade the eyes densely, either reserving the highlights or lifting them out with an eraser.

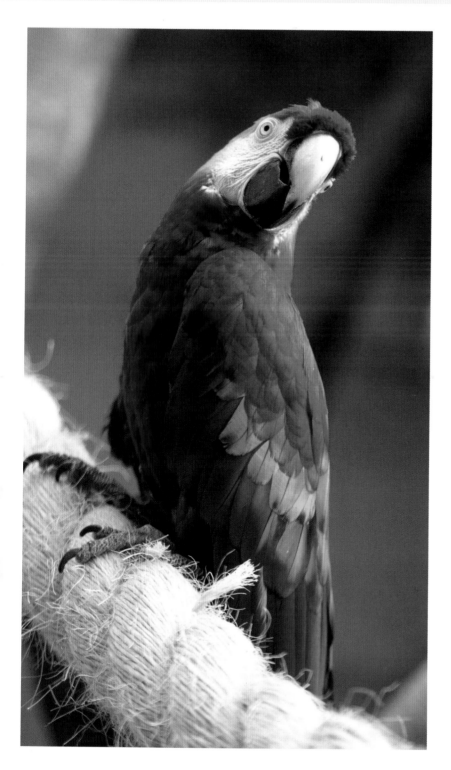

**Parrot** It could be helpful to enlarge this image, using a scanner or colour photocopier so that you can see the structure of the feathers more clearly. Tackle these and the fine hairs of the frayed rope with sharp pencils and sgraffito methods.

**Horse race** It is important to give a feeling of speed in your rendering, and you could do this by making vigorous hatched or shaded marks in the same direction as the horses' movement, from left to right. Carry this treatment through into the background, blending the marks to give a softer focus than that of the horses. Or you might like to work on the fine nuances of light and shade on the horse's coat, seen clearly in the close up, layering, compacting and burnishing your colour.

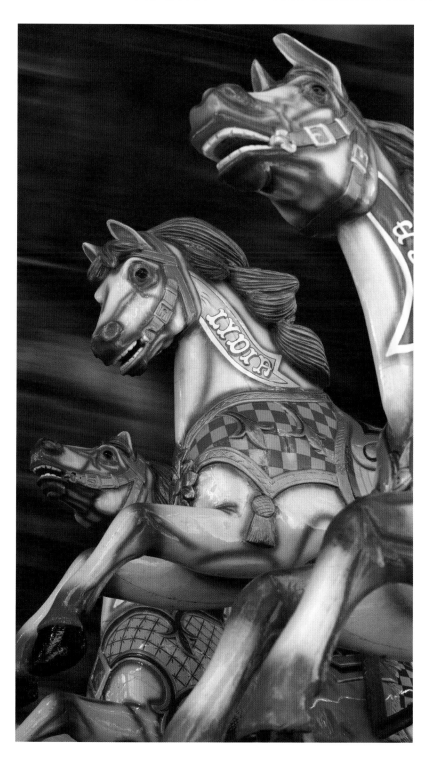

**Carousel horses** *Like the live horses, these painted and varnished creatures have a strong sheen, which can be achieved by careful blending and burnishing. Directional marks in the background will help to create the feeling of movement.*

# Still life

*Grapes* *You will need to use strong tone and colour contrasts to achieve this degree of vibrancy. The range of deep greens in the background will require several layers of densely shaded colour – dark reds, purple and indigo – to remove any vestige of white paper. Alternatively, a coloured paper could be used as a base for the layering, followed by maximum use of the lighter pinks, oranges and yellows for the fruit.*

**Melon slices** *You could experiment with just red, yellow and green pencils of various hues, with layering to obtain the intense shadows. Compacted layered colour would be best to suggest the background, which acts as a foil to the clear pinks and oranges in the foreground.*

### African basket and gourd

This subject offers the artist lovely textures to play with. Use an eraser as a tool to soften the relatively light-toned basket work – the removal of pigment being an integral part of the gradual build-up of tone and colour, as you define your work.

### Baked goods

You could describe the woven patterns of the basket and the texture of the wheat, bread and pastries using hatching and crosshatching techniques. Because of the relatively monochromatic colour of the subject, vary the tones with obvious changes in pressure and density.

# Buildings

**Reflected buildings** With an image as complex as this, you would need to trace the reflections in order to get everything in the right place. Start the colour work by putting in the main blocks of colour first and then overlay the shadows rather than colouring them separately. You may find an impressing tool with a fine point useful for the window grids of the office blocks.

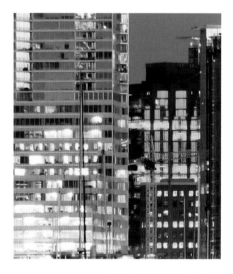

***Evening lights*** *Bright lights at twilight can make the sky seem a vivid blue, becoming deeper as the light fades. Make the most of the blue/orange complementary contrast to enhance the brightness by using dense shading or hatching for the lights and their reflections, or you could try using chalky oranges and yellows in light tones on a coloured paper.*

**Lighthouse at dusk** *Play around with different sizes and scales when planning your compositions. Here, the horizon is very low, and the lighthouse fills the space vertically, its height accentuated by the perspective that leads the eye upwards from almost ground level. You might try a coloured paper for this subject, working the orange and yellow very densely.*

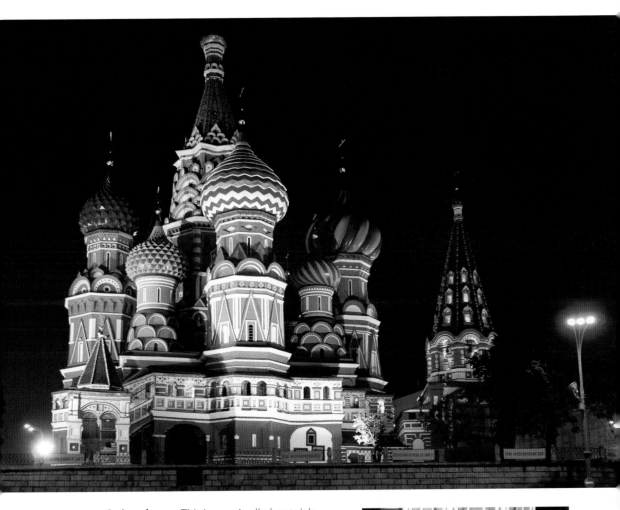

**Onion domes** *This image is all about rich colour and pattern, which need to be crisp and clear cut. If the scale of your work is small, your impressing tool should come in handy, used both at the initial drawing stage when the white of the paper will be incorporated and possibly later as well, for the green and yellow patterns.*

# Index

All materials and techniques are illustrated
Page numbers in *italics* refer to named drawings

# Credits

Quarto would like to thank and acknowledge the following for supplying the illustrations and photographs reproduced in this book:

Laura Duis: **72**; Emin Kuliyev/Shutterstock: **164**; Lazar Mihai-Bogdan/Shutterstock: **165**; Juriah Mosin/Shutterstock: **166**; Vova Pomortzeff/Shutterstock: **167**; Elena Elisseeva/Shutterstock: **169**; Alexphoto/Shutterstock: **170**; Bude Moha/Shutterstock: **171**; Myrthe Krook/Shutterstock: **172**; Photooiasson/Shutterstock: **173**; Afaizal/Shutterstock: **174**; Vladimir Sazonov/Shutterstock: **175**; Frank Ungrad/Shutterstock: **175**; Ben Heys/Shutterstock: **176**; Tatiana Morozova/Shutterstock: **177**; Jacqueline Abromeit/Shutterstock: **178**; Ronald Sumners/Shutterstock: **179**; Orientaly/Shuttestock: **180**; Elke Dennis/Shutterstock: **181**; N Joy Neish/Shutterstock: **182**; Magdalena Kucova/Shutterstock: **183**; Donald R. Swartz/Shutterstock: **184**; Hannamariah/Shutterstock: **185**; Florida Stock/Shutterstock: **186**; posztos/Shutterstock: **187**

Quarto would also like to thank the following contributing artists who are acknowledged beside their work:

Elisabeth Aubury
Robin Borrett (www.artistandillustrator.co.uk)
Graham Brace (www.grahambrace.com)
Susan Brooks (www.susanbrooksfineart.com)
Angela Cater (www.geocities.com/angelacater)
Katriona Chapman (www.iris-illustration.co.uk)
Richard Childs (www.chumleysart.com)
Vera Curnow (Veracurnow.com)
Laura Duis (ldart@earthlink.net)
Kendra Bidwell Ferreira (www.kjfdesign.com)
Jeff George (www.jeffgeorgeart.com)
Malcom Harrison

John Hayes (http://motornstuffart.co.uk/index.htm)
Mark Hudson
Dyanne Locati
Richard Lovesey (www.loveseyfineart.com)
Robert Maddison
Richard McDaniel (www.richardmcdaniel.com)
K. Scott McGregor (www.scottmcgregor.co.uk)
Angela Morgan
Mike Pease (mrpease@comcast.net)
Steve Taylor
John Townend
Peter Woof (www.axisweb.org/artist/peterwoof)

With special thanks to Derwent for kindly supplying the coloured pencils used and photographed in this book. For information on Derwent's products, visit: www.pencils.co.uk.